The
SCOTTISH
Football Book

No. 18

The SCOTTISH Football Book No. 18

Edited by
HUGH TAYLOR

STANLEY PAUL
London

STANLEY PAUL & CO LTD
3 Fitzroy Square, London W1

AN IMPRINT OF THE HUTCHINSON GROUP

London Melbourne Sydney
Aukland Johannesburg Cape Town
and agencies throughout the world
First published 1972

*This book has been set in Linotron Baskerville, printed in
Great Britain
by Flarepath Printers Ltd, St. Albans, Herts,
and bound by William Brendon, at Tiptree, Essex*

ISBN 0 09 112650 9

CONTENTS

The Editor says . . .

Although the 'Eurofirm' of Celtic and Rangers boosted our prestige in Europe, although the international scene looked brighter with the advent of the breezy Tommy Docherty as manager and although season 1971–72 had exciting moments, there is no doubt in my mind that all is not well with Scottish football.

Is there too much soccer? Unfortunately, there is far too much dull, ordinary football, football which makes the fans groan. Football in Scotland is glamorous and paying for the clubs at the top; for most of the others there is a struggle to make ends meet.

It is high time the top brass in Scottish football tried to stop the rot. For years, I have been crying out for streamlined leagues, for less bread-and-butter football and more variety. In vain. Scottish football struggles on. But under the present set-up I cannot see soccer as anything but a sick sport. When you think of clubs such as Dundee with only 5,000 supporters at their home games, you begin to wonder if there is any future for football in this country.

Football will falter until there is a super league here. The fans want action. And they would get it with a super-League of 12 or 14 clubs.

A new deal is needed, too, in relegation. We need three divisions, with four up and four down. But what a hope we have of improving football when far too many clubs don't care about progress and are happy to vegetate on their own little cabbage patch, giving nothing to the game but content to take their international tickets when the time comes.

In 1973, the Scottish Football Association will be 100 years old—but I wonder if the Association will last another 100 years? To be blunt, the First Division has become a farce. Celtic are so far out on their own that they can win the flag without looking round. We need a greater challenge. Even Celtic know that and manager Jock Stein would certainly welcome sterner competition. Aberdeen have tried hard. But they were second again. Now they have bought new strikers in Barry Mitchell, of Dunfermline, and Drew Jarvie, of Airdrie, and perhaps they will put more emphasis on attack in their new bid to topple the Celts.

Rangers tasted success in Europe but still they lagged at home, failing in all the domestic tournaments.

The frank truth is that without Celtic, Aberdeen and Rangers, however, Scotland, despite stout efforts in the Texaco Cup, which we have still to win, would be a Cinderella footballing country.

Yet we continue to produce some of the greatest players in the world and manager Docherty marvels at the steady stream of talent he can dip into for his international teams. To me, it seems crazy and almost criminal that such good players have to go to England to earn the money their ability demands. Why have we the natural talent to play and yet fail at the top to maintain a set-up which will keep football in Scotland prosperous?

Still, we'll battle on. Some clubs such as Kilmarnock have seen the light and gone part-time, because they know it's the only way to survive, And, of course, social clubs play a vital role in keeping the clubs alive. Who said we've made progress? In the old days, raffles were held to keep football going. We're back where we started. I wonder if ever football can exist—by playing the type of game which will bring back the fans who have deserted the terracings in droves.

All, though, wasn't black. There was the breath of fresh air Partick Thistle brought to the scene by winning the League Cup Final—their first major trophy for 50 years . . . and achieved in the season after they gained promotion.

There was the challenge of Eddie Turnbull, who will certainly do with Hibs what he did with Aberdeen: make them a team to worry Celtic, this time in the League. His fine work shows that at managerial, as well as at player level, Scotland is not short of first-class material.

It was sad to see Dunfermline, not so long ago rated with Kilmarnock as the teams most likely to upset the giants, go down to the Second Division with Clyde, who have also been noted in the recent past for neat soccer.

It was good to see persevering Arbroath and Dumbarton, one of the pioneering clubs and in their centenary year, win the stern battle for promotion.

Indeed, one of the bright sides is that football has improved dramatically in the Second Division.

A tremendous fear, however, is that trouble on the terracing is on the increase. Too many clubs have thugs and hooligans among their 'supporters'. Rangers paid a severe penalty for their fans' conduct in Spain. It may be a sign of the times that these idiots would rather cause a riot than watch peacefully. Nevertheless, the conduct of a minority is driving away the decent fans. And we simply cannot afford to lose spectators.

Anyhow, a warm welcome to this new Scottish Football Book. And thanks for your letters and comments. I look forward to hearing from you.

HUGH TAYLOR

8

WAR AT HAMPDEN

The international that died of *shame*

It was to have been the day of Scottish national rejoicing—the day of triumph over England, the auld enemy. Hopes had seldom been higher than on the windy afternoon of May 27, 1972 and as the 119,325 spectators filed into Hampden's grey stadium they felt disasters in the past were over, considered the new spirit and confidence of the boys in blue would bring an epic victory.

With the advent of Tommy Docherty as team manager, there was great enthusiasm. Scotland had beaten Ireland and Wales and needed only a point to win the home international championship. England had faltered, losing at their own Wembley to little Ireland. The scent of victory was in the air.

Alas for the high hopes. Alas for British football.

The international of 1972 between Scotland and England was a disgrace, a blot on football and the season ended in one of the most unpleasant matches between the two countries, with a snarl and a scowl and a bitter clash.

Everything went wrong for Scotland—and it was a pity red-shirted Italian referee Sergio Gonella was so lenient.

We all knew it would be a tough clash—but little did we think it would turn into a battle.

The teams were:
Scotland: Clark (Aberdeen), Brownlie (Hibernian), Donachie (Manchester City), Bremner (Leeds United—capt), McNeill (Celtic), Moncur (Newcastle United), Lorimer (Leeds), Gemmill (Derby County), Macari (Celtic), Law (Manchester United), Hartford (West Bromwich Albion).

England: Banks (Stoke City), Madeley (Leeds), Hughes (Liverpool), Storey (Arsenal), McFarland (Derby County), Moore (West Ham—capt), Ball (Arsenal), Bell (Manchester City),

9

Chivers (Tottenham Hotspur), Marsh (Manchester City), Hunter (Leeds).

Hardly had the match begun on a dreadful day for football, with the violent wind starching the flags to the poles, than the martial arts began and high tackles, wild kicks and brutal charges were taken as a matter of course.

Who was to blame? Undoubtedly England took a psychological advantage. They knew the Scottish temperament—and its failings. They felt that the menace of husky destroyers like Storey and Hunter would provoke the Scots, fiery bantam cocks, into retaliation. That is what happened. So no one took credit.

Scotland started promisingly enough. In the third minute John Brownlie, a magnificent young back, surprised even the redoubtable Gordon Banks with a high, dropping shot from the wing and the Scots claimed the ball was over the line as the keeper grasped it above his head.

Then the kicking started and the game became disgracefully physical. McFarland fouled the volatile Denis Law—and, was punched on the jaw. Hunter kicked Brownlie. Storey had a swing at Bremner. Ball felled Bremner from behind. And these were merely the principal fouls in a period of violence that had no place on any football field, far less an international arena.

Three players were cautioned, England's Ball and Scotland's McNeill and Hartford.

Matters became so bad that referee Gonella called the two captains together and asked them to calm their men. It made no difference.

It took nearly 25 minutes for the Hampden fans to see a real soccer move

and that was when Storey kicked off the line a shot from Hartford which had been deflected by Bremner and had deceived Banks.

Scotland were on top but were cynically stopped by sheer strength and they were spiteful in retaliation, although it was a case almost of boys against men.

Scotland, however, played neat, constructive football and Banks blocked a Lorimer effort. Then, in almost complete silence, England scored against the run of play—a goal, in the words of sad Tommy Docherty afterwards, like something out of Comic Cuts.

A bad pass by Bremner was intercepted by Ball and he and the massive Chivers combined well deep into the Scotland penalty area. Ball's final prod sent the ball under Clark's diving body and it rolled slowly over the line, with a posse of blue-clad defenders trying vainly to stop it.

Still the violence went on and there was a tackle on little Lou Macari which left the Celtic striker with his torn jersey flapping round his neck.

Now there was unease in the Scotland defence and Colin Bell, the best player on the field, had bad luck with a splendid shot which shaved the outside of the post.

Some of the poison drained out of the game in the second half, with England much less violent but the polluting effect of the earlier fouls were felt until the end.

Play was much better, with England

Trouble flares at Hampden as Billy McNeill is restrained after John Brownlie had been badly fouled.

10

Gritted teeth in the Scotland—England international with Lou Macari and Denis Law trying to make goalkeeper Gordon Banks the meat in the sandwich.

Again it's Banks to England's rescue with a flying save as the two raiders, Law and Macari, close in.

England centre-half Roy McFarland coolly breaks up a Scottish attack.

the more organised side. Yet Scotland went near in an exciting spell, with the irrepressible Law and Macari stirring up the action.

A great tackle by McFarland on Law saved a goal. Macari crossed from the left and a careful Law header was stopped by Hughes on the line. Banks hurt a hand as Hartford charged in.

Jinky Jimmy Johnstone was brought on for Archie Gemmill but it was too late and the Celt, who can be so brilliant, did not sparkle. Fifteen minutes from time manager Docherty made another change, taking off the clever left-back

Willie Donnachie and bringing on Tony Green.

This enabled Scotland to build neater play in the mid-field but the strong England defence held out. Sir Alf Ramsey took off Marsh and substituted MacDonald and near the end England almost scored again when Chivers, showing his massive authority, flicked a header just past the Scottish post.

Unfortunately, the game ended as

14

A happier Hampden occasion as Denis Law strikes in the game against Wales.

More Hampden joy as youngsters mob Peter Lorimer after scoring a goal.

unhappily as it began, with the petulant Alan Ball giving a two-finger gesture to the Scottish fans as he walked off the pitch.

It wasn't a game to remember and officials of both countries condemned the brutality. Said Sir Alf: 'I disliked the physical aspect intensely in the first 20 minutes. I think both teams wanted to win and there was rivalry between players from the same club on opposite sides and there is a great deal of feeling between them at club level.'

In the end, Scotland were probably unlucky to lose 1–0 but, frankly, neither side distinguished itself.

I felt that the presence in the England midfield of Storey and Hunter, two players not noted for their reluctance to hammer in physically, was seen by some of the Scots as an invitation to war.

Scotland fell into the trap. Unlike the West Germans, who had decisively beaten England and who disdained the savagery of their opponents in Berlin and kept on playing football, the Scots became war-like, retaliating with the old fervour of the 'Wha daur meddle wi' me' clans. That suited England perfectly. So there was little football.

There were 46 physical fouls recorded during the match—24 against England and 22 against Scotland.

And the sad truth was that Scotland failed where the team manager expected them to be strongest—in mid-field. There was no player of inspiration or class to vary the style, to bring imagination and a shrewd long pass, no Gray or Murdoch or Cooke who would have made a world of difference.

This deficiency was all the sadder because Scotland carried a real threat at the front. England's crowding defence gave Peter Lorimer little room for his explosive shooting to count. But Law, who became the hero of Hampden again with fine displays, was near his old electric self and Macari was sharp and energetic, a real find.

It was, however, the war at Hampden which will be remembered, not the good football and still Docherty's search for success had to go on.

On this form, neither Scotland nor England looked as though they had much chance of World Cup success and the fans were sick of what passes for football in this modern age.

The main aim of too many players seemed to be to hurt an opponent and because there were so many culprits on both sides it was impossible to aportion blame.

Once the Scotland–England international was an exhibition of all that was best in British football, hard but fair and sporting, with artists allowed to show their talent.

Now it's a battle, with a cluttered midfield and anyone trying to hold the ball ruthlessly chopped down.

In the end, Scotland were reduced to pumping high balls into the England penalty area, useless against the tall defenders.

Much more thought must go into our planning before we can say we are back in the ranks of the mighty footballing nations.

Real football has been the victim of the craze for the numbers racket, with command in the mid-field all, no matter how many players are told to form a phalanx there.

Hampden, 1972, was the worst advertisement British football has ever had.

The Doc's a tonic

Tommy Docherty brought a breath of fresh air into the musty corridors of Scottish football when he was appointed national team manager—and there seems little doubt that he will be the most successful of the line.

He's a tonic, the Doc—brisk, cheerful, enthusiastic. He's never at a loss for a quip. He likes his joke. For instance, of one player more noted for his clever play on the field than his intelligence off it, he said: 'That one doesn't know the meaning of the word, defeat. And there's a million other words he doesn't know the meaning of.' He's a player's man, though—and a journalist's man, a likeable, likely lad who gets on with everyone, apart from the old fuddy-duddies who have done so much to halt our soccer progress.

Controversy and Docherty, of course, go hand in hand. He breezes like a cyclone and sometimes he's apt to wear people out. But no-one can doubt his patriotism, his burning desire to put Scotland back on top of the football world.

One of his proudest moments came in season 1956–57 when he was made captain of Scotland. There was a row over that. At that time, Scotland were again on the way to the stars. Aye, again. . .

They had beaten Spain at Hampden in the World Cup qualifying series and won against Switzerland in Basle. Tommy Docherty was the outstanding player.

Then the trouble began. George Young, of Rangers and one of the truly great Scotland captains, was dropped for a friendly against Germany in Stuttgart. Docherty was made captain in his place and the Scots were inspired, beating the then World Cup holders 3–1.

But Young was dropped again for the match against Spain in Madrid. So was his Rangers' team-mate, Ian McColl, later to be a Scotland manager.

Many were shocked at the selectors' decision because the game in Spain would have been Young's last appearance. The heart seemed to have gone out of Scotland for they lost 4–1.

Again Docherty, however, was a splendid skipper. And he has always regarded that as his greatest honour in football. He has told me in his own ebullient way: 'For a Scottish player, it is simply terrific to be made captain of your country. Some people said the captaincy affected my play. Quite honestly, I never believed that. It's a responsible job but so great was the honour that I tried to play all the harder.'

When he retired from playing, Tommy Docherty became a manager, a famous, often successful but, again, invariably controversial, manager.

All that is in the past, though. The Doc is probably one of the happiest men in the game now—doing his best for Scotland.

Whether, of course, he will be the new Messiah won't be known for a long time.

In this modern age, no country can become as efficient or colourful as Brazil in months. It takes years to build a successful international side—but the Doc is going about it the right way. The contagious vitality of his personality is a great help. He is vigorous, deeply immersed in football, his faith in the Scottish footballer undying.

Wrong impression

And how he loves Scotland! He said: 'How else can you be but proud to be a Scot when you realise that we have more highly successful people per head of population than any other nation! Look at Alexander Fleming, David Livingstone, Jackie Stewart, Ken Buchanan—all great in their field. Others, like Sir Matt Busby and Sean Connery are world-famous. Every time a Scot takes on the world and wins I feel proud.'

Certainly Tommy Docherty will work like a slave, pull out every stop to make Scotland a top footballing nation again.

Many people have the wrong impression of Docherty, believing him to have been merely a hard, enthusiastic player, a foil mainly, or even protector, of the richly talented artist, Tom Finney.

Amazing tricks

They couldn't be more wrong. For that's a mistake too many make.

There was Davie Mackay, for instance. Again it was said of him that he was only a tough half-back. What rubbish! Mackay was also a brilliant ball worker.

He could do amazing tricks with a ball—or with a coin. You can't play in top-class soccer without being a talented ball worker. The Doc, too, had more, much more, than brawn.

Sure, Docherty was powerful. But he also read the game brilliantly, had deft touches and passed superbly. Now as Scotland's boss, he demands, first of all, skill, which, he feels, is the natural heritage of the Scottish player.

He says: 'To be a first-class footballer, one thing is essential above all others—ball control. To be able to control a football, no matter how it comes to you, hard or high, bumping or spinning, is the hallmark of a good player.'

'The advantages in having this skill are tremendous, especially in a high class of football, where defenders are fast and clever.'

Time to spare

'If he can kill a ball so that it stays with him, a player will give himself valuable split seconds in evading a tackle, looking for an unmarked team-mate or crashing a shot for goal.'

'This is the secret behind the expression, "he looks as though he has all the time in the world", which is often used to describe great players of all ball games. The fact is that they do have time to spare, not "all the time in the world" but seconds which are valuable in a fast game like football. A good player makes this time for himself by his ability to cushion the ball with any part of his body, head, chest, thighs and feet. He has only developed this skill through constant practice with a ball since he was a boy.'

Of course, Scots being the argumentative types they are and the greatest (so we imagine) soccer experts in the world, Docherty's tactics will be questioned. But I know our international future is in good hands. Behind the Doc's comedian's façade lies a brilliant football brain. And he can also get over to his players his ideas—in language they understand and like.

Tommy Docherty has now been more than ten years in the chair as manager. He has had experience at all levels, manager of Chelsea, Rotherham, Queen's Park Rangers, Aston Villa, Oporto, in Portugal. He has learned lessons the hard way. He says:

'I know now that any problems which arise should be dealt with just between myself and the people concerned. Sometimes news reaches the public first and upsets people.'

'As far as players are concerned, I have found the better the player the bigger the problem he is. But it's up to the manager to try to sort out those problems.'

Already Tommy Docherty has given Scotland a tonic. Already his tactics are producing results. Already our stock has risen at international level.

There may be a long way yet to go—but Docherty has also the faith of his players. Listen to Scottish captain Billy Bremner:

'Again it's just wonderful to play for Scotland. We're all excited about it. Docherty has us organised at last. He's a great boss, the man who can lead us to the top.'

Already he has been accused of fielding too many mid-field players—but it's all part of the new Docherty pattern. Tommy's a man who knows his own mind.

He likes multi-purpose players but he insists that these players have talent. 'That's why they're so good, that's why they can play anywhere if needed,' He says.

Already there's a great new spirit, thanks to the Doc.

There may be failures—but Scotland are well on the way back to greatness . . . thanks to the Doc.

The Tainted Glory

SHAME IN SPAIN AS RANGERS TRIUMPH IN EUROPE

Rangers on the night of May 24, 1972, at last won the trophy they had been seeking for more than a decade – and the triumph was sweet. But the famous Ibrox club's wonderful feat of taking the European Cup-winners Cup by beating old rivals, Moscow Dynamo, in the Barcelona final was marred by disgraceful conduct by their supporters.

And shame in Spain followed the finest night in Rangers' history.

Nothing, however—not even a two-year ban imposed later by UEFA—can take away from the way Rangers played in taking the trophy their traditions demanded. Their team gave everything for glory.

Rangers won the cup the hard way—just as they had to do everything the hard way on their way to the final, in ties in which they beat some of the best clubs in Europe.

More than 20,000 fans from Scotland had made the trip to Barcelona to cheer on their heroes and they saw the teams line up for the final like this:

Rangers: McCloy, Jardine, Mathieson, Greig, Johnstone, Smith, McLean, Conn, Stein, MacDonald, Johnston.

Moscow Dynamo: Pilgui, Basalacev, Dolmatov, Dolbonossov, Juvok, Baidachnyi, Jakubik, Sabo, Mahovikov, Evrizhin.

Referee: Jose Mendibi, Spain.

Rangers paid tremendous respect to the Russians when the game began. Then it became clear that the Russians were hard and honest but hardly spectacular and not all that speedy. Rangers found fluency.

In 24 minutes they took the lead with a fine move, started, predictably, by Dave Smith, the coolest man on the pitch. He pushed a long ball into the heart of the Russian defence. And Colin Stein scored a magnificent goal.

The centre-forward chased the ball and although he seemed crowded out by Dynamo defenders he got a toe to it and scored with a fine shot.

That was what Rangers needed. John Greig, who had been out of action through injury for weeks, was an inspiration. Smith and young Derek Johnstone were brilliant.

Rangers moved slowly but surely towards the trophy they had been seeking for a long, long time. And they scored a fine second goal just before half-time.

It was almost a replica of the first. Rangers had discovered the weak link in the Russian defence. Again Smith the calm beautifully slanted a ball into the penalty area. This time Willie Johnston finished the move with a flashing header which flew past Pilgui into the net. A goal from the text-book.

The fans were delirious as the Rangers left the field at half-time. And the cup

Valiant goalkeeper Peter McCloy in action.

was fated to go to Ibrox as Johnston scored his team's third goal.

Tall Peter McCloy, so reliable in goal, set up the move with a huge punt into the Russian half. It was pursued by Johnston, so quick and brave. As the Russians seemed to stand still, the Rangers winger hit the ball into the net from the middle of the penalty area.

And then the rejoicing had to stop.

John Greig was booked for a foul on Sabo. Dynamo took off Jakubik and replaced him with Eschtrekov. And a moment of carelessness in the 59th minute was expensive for the Scots when the substitute, an outstanding player, scored.

The Ibrox defence was too casual as Jardine missed a tackle and left Evrizhin in possession out on the right wing.

The ball was chipped in towards goal and as McCloy came out to narrow the angle the Dynamo winger squared to Eschtrekov, with the Rangers defence in a tangle, and it was just too easy for the Moscow man to score.

The time for glory was running out and with three minutes left Rangers lost another goal.

23

Rangers' captain John Greig drives on.

Mahovikov lobbed the ball simply into the net from 10 yards with McCloy off his line.

Then came the tragedy for Rangers—the tragedy of their fans.

For supporters decked out in the blue favours fought a pitched battle with baton-swinging Spanish police. It was the fifth time the fans had scurried madly onto the great Barcelona pitch from their seats on the steep tiers of concrete. Finally, the pistol-packing security police, who had shown total apathy before, lost their heads at the end of the game. They charged into the crowd with batons swinging madly. Fans were bludgeoned to the ground. Then came the most astonishing scene of all, with hordes of yelling Scottish fans leaping from the terracing to chase the police halfway across the pitch in disorder.

Other supporters hurled cushions and bottles. The police took some of the blame.

For half an hour before the kick-off the fans were given the freedom of the pitch. When the Rangers team tried to come on with the Russians just behind them, the fans ran on in a crazed show of adulation.

It took ten minutes to restore order and Rangers manager Willie Waddell had to plead with the mob to go off. When Stein scored the first goal, thousands again ran onto the field. And it happened again when Willie Johnston scored the second goal.

Just before the end of the game the fans misread a signal by the referee when he raised his hand for a foul. They thought he was ending the match and on they came again in whooping droves.

Then there was the final mud-bath finish. Delirious with joy, the thousands of Scots invaded the field—and they robbed Rangers captain Greig of the chance of being publicly handed the handsome trophy.

It was a tragedy that the hooligans, crazed with drink and emotion, should have ruined Rangers' greatest night.

For there were repercussions.

Rangers' glory had been tarnished—and the fans were to blame.

If the match had been played at home, the trouble would never have developed. The Glasgow police would have handled the situation with more forbearance for, after all, at practically every big European final the supporters of the winning team have been allowed to overflow the pitch to see their idols receive the trophy.

The Spanish police were brutal and inconsistent. But complaints about them are no excuse for when they are abroad football fans should respect the ways of the country and they might have known that the police of Spain did not stand on ceremony with demonstrators or exuberant supporters.

It will be a long time before the shocking conduct of the fans is forgotten and it was not the first display of hooliganism by the Ibrox camp-followers, who had disgusted people in Newcastle particularly by the aftermath of a match there.

It can be said that football attracts a hooligan minority of low intelligence, poorly educated, brought up in slums and whose partisanship is inflamed by drink.

It was not the fault of Rangers that their fans let them down.

But the problem is how to restrain the folly of a large number of irresponsible youth, excited by victory and alcohol.

It is sad that Scots fans are at their worst outside their own country.

The disgraceful conduct cost Rangers dear—and how sad that the fans were so stupid on the club's most magnificent night.

Up-and-coming—that's Derek Johnstone, the bright young Ranger.

The legend of Dixie Deans

It made a sad night for Celtic, but in Scotland the champions marched on

It is hardly surprising that the folk-lore of Scottish football is filled with legends tinged with tragedy. That, after all, is the history of Scotland, grim, sad stories of a little nation fighting valiantly but so often fruitlessly against the odds. Tears and laments have been more often our legacy than the heady spice of triumph. 'Wae is me' is the phrase for too many dismal occasions in Scottish life: the

beheading of Mary Queen of Scots, the defeat of Bonnie Prince Charles, the death of a king at Flodden, the massacre of Glencoe, the ill-fated Darien scheme.

In football, too, it is tragedy that we remember: the dreadful blunder of Motherwell's Alan Craig when he headed into his own goal and lost his team a cup final against Celtic they seemed certain to win, the shot Hearts'

Willie Bauld hit against the cross-bar at Hampden and so stopped Scotland going to a World Cup in Rio, disasters against England at Wembley.

And, on the night of April 19, 1972, Dixie Deans, of Celtic wrote himself a new chapter in Scotland's sad soccer history.

Dixie, transferred only that season from Motherwell and playing in his first big European Cup-tie, missed a penalty—and Celtic once again plunged out of the European Cup after more than two hours of slogging work, frustration and heartbreak.

Once again, too, an ice-cool Italian team, this time Inter-Milan, gaining revenge for their European Cup final by the Scottish champions in Lisbon, shattered the Celtic dream of glory.

It happened when Celtic were once again on top of the world. It happened on one of the greatest nights even in the history of Glasgow, that football-crazy city.

It happened on the night that Glasgow, a city of less than one million inhabitants, had, for the second time in a season, more than 150,000 people watching football at the same time. Of course, Glasgow holds practically every soccer record—the biggest crowd ever to pay for a match in Britain, the 149,547 who watched Scotland play England in 1937, the 146,433 that same season who attended the Scottish Cup Final between Celtic and Aberdeen, the 265,199 who saw the two games in the Rangers v Morton Scottish Cup Final in 1948, the record crowd for a European Cup Final in 1960 when 127,621 were at Hampden for the Real Madrid-Eintracht game.

Now the vast crowds had turned up at Parkhead and Ibrox for the European

Dixie Deans, missed a vital penalty against Inter-Milan—but did a fine job for the champions with many great goals.

Cup-tie between Celtic and Inter-Milan and the Cup-winners game between Rangers and Munich Bayern.

Celtic had surprised Europe. Manager Jock Stein had waved his magic wand and cast a spell which gave Parkhead a team of all the talents. Stein hadn't really expected to go so far in Europe. His Lisbon team had broken up and he had brought in new young faces. But they had blended well and, with new methods, with skill and organisation thoughtfully blended, had reached the semi-final of the premier competition, had outmanoeuvred those masters of tactics, Inter Milan, in a no-scoring draw in the first leg at the San Siro stadium in Milan.

Celtic were on the crest of the wave, having already beaten B 1903 of Copenhagen, Sliema Wanderers of Malta and Ujpest Dosza of Hungary in the previous rounds.

So was Dixie Deans, an able striker who had been on the goal trail since joining Celtic and who now had achieved his ambition by playing in a European semi-final.

Once again, however, it turned out to be tragedy for Celtic—in a tense, dramatic finish in which penalty kicks decided the tie.

After the longest night of the year for the 75,000 fans it was still 0–0. Celtic had pressed remorselessly, relentlessly—but extra time had come and gone and it was still 0–0. And then came Parkhead's most nerve-wracking moment. Each team had to take five penalty kicks.

Sandro Mazzola, the imperturbable Inter Milan skipper, stepped up to take the first kick. Neatly, coolly, he flicked it in at the far corner of the net, past the despairing hands of Celtic goalkeeper,

Davie Hay, one of the powerful young Celtic players. He was injured and thus badly missed in the match against Inter-Milan.

Evan Williams. Inter were one up on penalties.

Now it was the dreadful moment of truth for Dixie Deans, who had come on as a substitute for Kenny Dalglish.

To his utter anguish, Dixie blasted the ball high over the bar.

And that, Celtic fans, realised, was that.

It was.

For the technically-perfect Inter would not, they knew, miss this chance. They didn't. Facchetti scored—so did Frustalupi, and Pellizzaro and Jair. For Celtic, Craig, Johnstone, McCluskey and Murdoch were bang on the target—but it was too late. Celtic were out 5–4 on penalties.

Poor Deans. He will go down in history. But, to be fair, it wasn't really his fault that Celtic went out. It was really a night of tragic anti-climax for the champions. For most of the match they hammered the Italian goal. But they lacked the flair, the imagination, the know-how which had taken them through to the semi-final. And the longer the match went on the cooler grew the brilliant Inter defence.

Towards the end there was more than a tinge of desperation in the Celtic raids. Indeed, only in the opening 20 minutes did they look their real selves.

Driven on by the mighty Bobby Murdoch, their outstanding player, Celtic swarmed down from the start on Vieri in the Inter goal. A selection of the old magical moves had the crowd shouting with glee.

The fans thought a goal had to come. The Italians had different ideas. Superbly drilled by the veterans Facchetti and Burgnich, they found great poise—and in the end Celtic were a frustrated side.

Their tragedy was that they failed to produce their real form when they needed it most—and so they were out of Europe.

Defeat was all the more bitter as across the city at Ibrox Rangers had won through to the final of the European Cup-winners Cup by beating Munich Bayern in the second leg of an exciting semi-final.

But there were no moans from Celtic. Of course, it was disappointing. But Celtic were still Scotland's No 1 team. Indeed, it seemed during the season, in which they dominated, that they were out of their class. They were worthy champions once again, a great team who would grow even greater. And they played football, attacking football.

Their defeat in the European Cup semi-final was much less of an injustice than Inter's victory. If Celtic lacked the sparkle and wit needed on that night, the Italians were shamefully devoid of ambition and honesty of purpose that should attend entry into the final of the greatest of all club tournaments.

And it is time these games, especially at this level, were played to a finish. That their contest was settled in the end by a disembodied series of penalties was a farcical deviation from the standards that should be found in the highest sphere of soccer.

In future, it must be a rule that drawn semi-finals in the top European competitions be decided on the play-off principle.

Inter's display, however, was a cruel defeat for real football for they devalued the European Cup. Earlier, they had lost 7–1 to Borussia Munchengladbach but had protested that a can had been thrown at one of their players. The result—a dreadful decision by EUFA

29

this—was overturned and Inter went on to the next round under false pretences, after beating the upset Germans.

Worse than that were the Italian tactics. They have talent in plenty but choose to exasperate everyone with their concentration on defence. To them, nothing matters but victory.

The grave danger is that this success of the Italians will influence others—and, unhappily, Inter's example is easier to imitate than most.

Thank goodness there is still plenty of life left in Celtic. They had too many stars injured on the night of the Inter game to be at full strength, yet still did most of the attacking. And they have excellent young players coming through. Frankly, they still look the greatest team in Scotland—and will be for many a long year to come.

What can you say about them? I am often accused of giving too much space to Celtic. What else can I do? Celtic claim it all . . . on merit.

And Dixie Deans will get over his penalty miss. He has scored great goals for his new team. The legend may live on—but Deans will make others, I'm sure. As he did in the Scottish Cup Final.

Celtic, too, will go on fighting to achieve their No 1 ambition—to win the world club championship by beating South American opponents.

They are the Scottish club most likely to succeed.

The teams at Parkhead for the European Cup semi-final were: Celtic—Williams, Craig, McCluskey, Murdoch, McNeill, Connelly, Johnstone, Dalglish, Macari, Callaghan, Lennox; Sub: Deans. Inter-Milan—Vieri, Bellugi, Facchetti, Oriali, Gubertoni, Burgnich, Jair, Bedin, Bertini, Mazzola, Frustalupi; Sub: Pelizzaro. Referee: Rudi Glockner, East Germany.

Lou Macari was another Celt who earned fame last season with scintillating displays in the attack.

None but the brave deserve the honour of Player of the Year

Dave Smith, Rangers' elegant sweeper, is Scotland's Player of the Year for season 1971–72.

Combine bravery with the skill of a master craftsman—and you get the Player of the Year, Dave Smith, elegant Rangers sweeper. Certainly Dave was a popular choice when he was named as top star by the Scottish Football Writers' Association for season 1971–72.

He met stiff opposition, though, for it was a good season for players. Second came Joe Harper, Aberdeen's ace of goal-scorers, and also competing strongly were Celtic's George Connelly, another master of defence, and Ken Dalglish, who had started the season so well, and Kilmarnock's fine young goalkeeper, Alistair Hunter.

The award to Smith was the culmination of a great fight. Twice he has shrugged off serious injuries. He broke a leg against Kilmarnock in 1970 and again a year later, this time at training.

But Dave is nothing if not brave. He returned to action against his old club, Aberdeen, in September, 1971, and since then he has been a key figure in the Rangers' ranks, playing a vital role in their European march in the Cup-winners Cup.

Smith typifies the thoughtful, talented Scottish player. He is never flurried, never worried. He always seems to have all the time in the world. He is never rash and while he is superb at breaking up opposing attacks he plays a big part in starting Rangers' raids with well-judged passes.

Rangers skipper John Greig sums up the Smith saga best. He said simply: 'Dave has never played better than in season 1971–72. Not only can he be one of the best attacking wing-halfs in the country he is also a great sweeper. He's a

31

natural player and the secret of his success is his reading of the game.'

Dave Smith is one of football's quiet men—and one of the game's gentlemen, a player who is an example to all aspiring lads. He likes the artistic side of the game, the elegant things of life—and that is reflected in the way he plays. He never retaliates, no matter how badly he is fouled. It would be the sensation of the century if he were ever booked or spoken to by a referee.

'Playing the game', though, runs in the Smith family. Dave's brother, Doug, who has been more than 15 years in the game as a centre-half with Dundee United, has never been in trouble either.

Dave has a simple philosophy. It is: 'If opponents want to prove themselves by being rough and tough, let them. I rely on what talent I have to prove myself. If I'm kicked or fouled, I ignore it. Anyhow, it's foolish to retaliate for it's the crime most likely to lead to bookings or even an ordering-off.'

Football is Dave's life. He thinks about it all the time—which is why he has been the idol of the Ibrox fans who love his cool approach. Sometimes he makes his supporters gasp for often his action is anything but classical. But seldom is Smith in trouble and he is wonderful at working himself out of tight situations.

Dave Smith brings distinction to the Scottish game—on and off the field. He has the touches of the old masters in this modern age of method—and he stands out as one of the best-liked exponents of football as well as a man of remarkable courage and determination.

Joe Harper, who scored 50 goals in season 1971–72, is also a young man who is loved by the fans. The men on the terracing want goals—and Joe, former Morton attacker, is just the man to get them.

The Aberdeen striker is one of the most dangerous players in football and that fact is recognised by opponents, who often delegate two defenders to try to mark him out of the game—and fail.

Alas for Joe, he also came second for Scotland. Despite his tremendous goal-scoring feats, he has been ignored for the international team.

'I'm desperate to play for my country,' says Joe, 'and I've never worked harder than I have this season. But I'm bitterly disappointed that I've not been chosen.'

In his nine years as a senior, Harper has made only two international sides, at Under-23 level against Wales and in a League national against Ireland.

Joe was on the mark against Ireland, scoring two goals, but he is now the forgotten man of the international scene.

But he had a wonderful record, having—at the end of last season—scored 78 goals in 121 games for Aberdeen since 1969. And it's all due to instinct and hard work.

Says Joe: 'It's important to be in the right place at the right time but that's something you can't learn or acquire. It's something that's just there. At Pittodrie, we put a lot of emphasis on shooting practice and that's helped me.

'It means hard work but in front of goal and under pressure there are rarely second chances. It's then that sharpness counts.'

Well, Joe Harper was second in season 1971–72. He's hoping he'll go one better this season. And no-one will work harder for honours than Joe Harper, the man with dynamite in his boots.

With a little help from my friends, the boss— and myself

He could be a pop star—modern, handsome, smiling, stylish. But he's a football star—Alan Rough, Partick Thistle's impressive young goalkeeper.

You might not think so, when you see the soccer stars in brilliant action, cheered by thousands, the sporting world at their feet, rejoicing in their superlative skill . . . but even these idolised players go off form, worry and know that, like everyone else, they are only human.

How do they recover? As the Beatles said, they can do with a little help from their friends. Sometimes, too, their bosses lend a helping hand. Most often, the helping hand has to come from—themselves. The stars, too, are hero-worshippers. They study players whom they think are the best in the world.

And it's when you hear great Scots talking enthusiastically of their heroes, saying these stars can never really be emulated, that you realise big-headedness isn't at all prevalent in our football circles.

Take Partick Thistle's Alan Rough, for instance, one of the finest goalkeepers we've had in years. Everything is going for him. He's a handsome youngster, dressing in mod gear. He has his own fan club, with members from as far afield as Inverness and Sweden, never mind Maryhill. Kids clamour for his autograph.

But Alan is as modest as he was when he joined up at Firhill, wondering how he was ever chosen to become a professional.

What he most dearly desires is to become as proficient as his idol, Peter Bonetti, the 'Cat' of Chelsea. 'I try to model my style on Bonetti,' says Alan, 'for he's a terrific goalkeeper, with fantastic reaction and mobility.'

A star from even further away from

33

Scotland is considered the greatest by East Fife winger, Billy McPhee. The name: Rivelino, the Brazilian attacker with the touch of magic.

'I have always been a keen student of the game,' says Billy, 'and I like to experiment with dead-ball situations. Then I watched Rivelino on television. That was a revelation. How Rivelino managed to get swerve on the ball showed that practice was everything. So I began to practise bending balls round defensive walls.'

And Billy has become an expert of an art rare in this country.

I feel it is a pity, though, that none of our current crop of players saw a man who could have given even Rivelino lessons. I refer to Alan Morton, the wee blue devil of Scotland and Rangers, who died in the winter of 1971.

But Alan's fame lives on. He was probably the greatest football genius this country produced. And his words on the game he distinguished should be listened to by every aspiring player. Alan was a fanatic for practice—and he became so brilliant that he could slice or hook at will. Here is the Morton formula for soccer success, words he spoke to me in an interview many, many years ago but still as important now as they were then, especially for anyone who hopes to be real players:

'There are three essentials for any young fellow who wants to become a footballer—balance, control and quickness off the mark. It has been said that I possessed these virtues but if they were revealed in my play they came to me only because of intensive practice.

'As a youth, I took a ball into the back garden and there, for hours, I practised. Behind our house and positioned in the back garden was a wooden door through which coal was emptied into the cellar. The door was four feet from ground level and in its centre was an opening just big enough to take a football. That was my target.

'I aimed to put the ball through that aperture. Of course, it didn't always

Here's Rough in action, making a fine save in a match against Dunfermline Athletic. A save as good as any his hero, Peter Bonetti, ever made.

work out that way. Sometimes, indeed, I didn't want a bullseye. It was often better when the ball came back from the wall at different angles. This meant that as the ball shot back off the wall I found myself forced to meet the return with either foot.

'Gradually I found myself kicking the ball in the direction I wanted. Proficiency came slowly but in a way that became natural the longer I kept at it. At first, it was all deliberate, but later it became almost automatic, a reflex action.

'Time meant nothing. I would hit the ball with my right foot. The ball would rebound from the wall at great speed, forcing me to anticipate its flight and make me dash to the other end of the lawn to meet it, this time with my left foot.

'This not only developed speed in gathering the ball but control in direction and in placing it to the mark. When I became a player, I had no difficulty in meeting a running ball and sending it where I wanted with either foot. That's all vital in disorganising a defence.

'If a defence is to be beaten, no time must be given to let the backs take up position to meet the attack. If once an opening has been made and the defenders caught off balance, a delay by the winger in crossing the ball, with colleagues up and ready to meet it, could enable a defender to travel eight to ten yards in a second. So you can see how vital it is to get a moving ball over with either foot without having to stop it first, thereby braking the attack and giving the defenders a chance they shouldn't be getting.'

There you are, then, aspiring wingers—more than a little help from the greatest outside left of them all.

It was sad that Torry Gillick, another

Rangers' Derek Johnstone (right), **the tall youngster with the great future, celebrates a goal against East Fife. A little help from manager Willie Waddell put Derek back on the goal-scoring trail.**

great Rangers player, died at around the same time as his famous predecessor, Alan Morton.

Gillick was one of football's most renowned characters. And the Ibrox manager, Willie Waddell, told me: 'Not only was Torry my left leg when we played on the same wing, he had a wonderful sense of humour. He could always cheer me up when I felt depressed and, being such a knowledgeable player, he could always tell me how to get out of my bad spells.'

Perhaps the most famous story about Gillick concerns the Moscow Dynamo, who played at Ibrox just after the war.

Torry told me it was the most dramatic and grimmest game of his career. It was so intense that no-one noticed at one point that the Dynamo were playing twelve men. Indeed, they might have had that extra man on all the time if it hadn't been for the fact that Torry suddenly realised he had two 'jailers', as he called them.

From the whistle, the Russian left-half had made himself Torry's bodyguard. This was a comparatively new move, for the tactics of this modern age hadn't been put into operation by British teams in the middle 1940's. Anyhow, Torry's close-marking pal tramped on his toes, jostled with elbows and kept breathing down his neck.

It was highly exasperating. What did you do? I asked Gillick. With that endearing smile crumpling up his rather sad face, Torry told me how he got his consolation. 'I cursed him from start to finish,' he said. 'But even that lost its charm for the Russian only laughed. He didn't understand a word of Scottish.'

Then Torry found he could move neither backwards nor forwards. Another Russian had joined the posse. Torry said he felt like the meat in a sandwich and he began to wonder where Dynamo were getting all the men from.

So he stopped short, almost making the two Russian markers bump into each other, and started to count the number of Rangers' opponents.

Right enough, there were twelve.

The Moscow men seemed to know what Torry was doing for as soon as he approached the referee one of them sneaked off the field.

That improved Rangers' chances—but it didn't help Torry much for his Russian jailer was still bang on top of him. Once, though, he came too close. As Torry kicked the ball, the Russian jammed in his leg and Torry had no chance to avoid it. That certainly stopped his smile.

But it almost caused an international incident at the banquet after the match. As the teams entered the dining room, the Russian left-half spotted Torry and began howling. He gestured, indicating his ankle, which was swollen like a balloon.

'When he pointed at me,' chuckled Torry, 'I thought he was going to burst me like a balloon. But it all ended in a friendly way.'

'With a little help,' Torry added, 'from a tot or two of vodka. . . .'

Nowadays, it's Willie Waddell who has to give a helping hand—and up-and-coming Derek Johnstone has to thank his boss for taking him out of a lean spell.

During the season, Derek lost his goal-scoring touch. What to do? said Derek: 'I was playing badly with the reserves. So badly indeed that I thought I was going to be dropped from the reserve side, which would have been a sore blow, especially as I had played so often in the first team.'

Then—in stepped Willie Waddell. He took Derek into his office at Ibrox and told him he felt he needed a better understanding of the game.

From a new viewpoint.

Said Willie: 'Try to see your leader's role from the centre-half position.'

Derek was played at centre-half and made a hit, both in the first and second teams.

But although he has been hailed in Scotland as the new John Charles, Derek seems fated to earn real fame as an attacker. And when the emergency arose up front and Derek came back he showed his spell in the defence had sharpened his goal-scoring appetite.

Thanks to the boss.

Is Football Too Tough?

The noble Lord had a word for it.

Every time I hear a complaint about football becoming too rough, I smile. For I look back to the dawn of the game as we know it today, study the old books and think about how tough football was in the days of yore.

For instance, there is a true story about Lord Kinnaird, a famous player with the Old Etonians. Arthur Kinnaird was well-known for his hacking. And when the President of the Football Association, Sir Francis Marindin, called one afternoon on Kinnaird's mother, he found her worried about her son.

'I'm afraid,' she said, 'that one of these days Arthur will come home with a broken leg.'

Said Marindin: 'I shouldn't worry about that, if I were you, Ma'am. It won't be his own.'

That was away back in 1880—a year in which the new humanism of the times was evinced in the passing of a law prohibiting a player from charging his opponent by leaping on him. And what Kinnaird said about this, I shudder to think. For it was the noble lord who was the principal character in another of football's immortal stories. Kinnaird also played for the Wanderers and he took part in nine F.A. Cup Finals for his team and for the Old Etonians. He wore a long white jersey, tight white trousers and cricket cap and sported a blazing red beard, which must have struck terror into the hearts of opponents.

So fierce was Kinnaird that he upset even C. W. Alcock, the first Homeric figure in the game, who is recorded as delighting in W. G. Grace's appearance in football because he bowled over his opponents like Catherine Wheels.

In one game Kinnaird captained a side against Alcock's and was asked: 'Shall we play fair—or shall we have hacking?'

'Oh, let's have hacking,' cried his Lordship—and they did.

Soccer was no game for cissies in the early days and there was opposition in the middle 1800's when a Cambridge pioneer, J. C. Thring, set down the first set of rules for universal adoption. Called the 'Code of the Simplest Game,' it had in Rule 3 this charming statement: 'Kicks must be aimed only at the ball.'

And 'Never mind the ball, get on with the game' must have been the motto then. Many legislators were against the banning of hacking and Mr. Morley, secretary of the F.A., was reported as saying:

'I think that the hacking is more dreadful in name and on paper than in reality.'

But Mr. Morley was against hacking because 'If we have hacking, no-one who has arrived at the years of discretion will play at football and it will be entirely

relinquished to schoolboys.'

A Mr. Campbell, of the F.A., had this to say: 'Hacking is the true football game and if you look into the Winchester records you will find that men were so wounded that two of them were actually carried off the field.

'As to not liking hacking . . . that savours far more of the feelings of those who like their pipes and grog or schnapps more than the manly game of football. I think they object to hacking because too many members of clubs began late in life and were too old for that spirit of the game which was so fully entered into at the public schools. . . .

'If you do away with hacking, you will do away with all the courage and pluck of the game and I will be bound to bring over a lot of Frenchmen who would beat you with a week's practice.

'We all like running and hacking and will not play any other game.'

Certainly the brutality of the early days has gone. But still the arguments rage: Is football too tough? One of Scotland's greatest players, Willie Ormond, had this to say last season about the game: 'As manager of St. Johnstone, I think the football in Scotland is too physical for my team to win honours at home, though I feel we can do well in Europe.'

And many legislators in Scotland felt that the revolution which had taken place in England should spread to Scotland. But—was it a revolution in England, where tackling had become almost a terrorist's weapon and the fouls were alarming to those who were watching an English game for the first time?

The truth was that there had been no revolution; nothing had changed in England—except that, and not before time, the laws were being more strictly and uniformly enforced. Indeed, the initial outcry by players and managers was a measure of how much latitude had been allowed in the past and how frequently the rules were being flouted.

Football in England was becoming the realm of the clogger—so the kicking had to stop before the game was hacked to death in season 1971–72.

The whole character of the game needed to be changed. On the field, it was a game of goal-stopping, last-ditch defensiveness, of brute force, relieved by such trickery as shamming injury and a refusal to accept referees' decisions without arguments and protests.

Well, England stopped it, stopped the appalling deterioration of sportsmanship, stopped the action of clubs who had a clogger intent only on putting a clever opponent out of a match.

Should Scotland, then, have a purge?

Not at all. Sure, there are hard men in our game—there always have been. There are the actors. There are the petulant schoolboys. And now and again we see powerful players trying to intimidate opponents.

And there is little doubt that the game has become less sporting, mainly because in these modern times there is so much at stake.

Frustration also plays a part in the deterioration of the character of the game.

Despite the spectacular play of teams such as Celtic, Rangers and St. Johnstone, the tendency is toward even stronger defensive tactics. Systems expressed by formulas such as 1–4–3–3, 1–4–4–2, 1–1–4–2–3 have meant an increase of the number of players in defence. So the number of players in defence prevailed over the number of forwards, thus breaking the numerical

Close marking—that's all in the game today. Here you see Rangers' Ronnie McKinnon keeping a tight grip on Celtic's John Hughes, now with Crystal Palace.

balance in teams established over the last few decades.

There were fewer stars, practically no new superstars. Combined offensive style became almost impossible. Thus the number of goals was reduced and football became less attractive.

Indeed, football became nearly a science and science is cold-blooded. No wonder Scottish players, who thrive on the artistic, the imaginative and the spectacular, sometimes lost their heads.

Not many, I grant you. Scotland can still be proud of its footballers. Most of our teams would rather go out for glory.

But unless there is a break in the fetish for defence, for cutting down good teams to the minnow size of too many opponents, there will be a continued decrease in sportsmanship—and even our Scottish soccer may require a purge.

I feel our referees should allow greater freedom to our ball players—and no country has more entrancing artists—so that the spectators can see more attractive football.

But we must all face the fact that football has changed. No longer can we afford to be romantic idealists, bringing a breath of intellectualism to the game. Method must be welded to free expression, whether we like it or not. Close marking is here to stay.

But as long as it remains close and not dirty I won't complain.

So the job of the referee is tougher. He must make up his mind from the start of a game what is fair marking and what isn't.

Scotland, though, is gradually making the best of both worlds of football—the old and the new. And my sincere opinion is that the game hasn't changed all that much—in its sporting spirit—since the old days.

Is football too tough? No, says Colin Stein, of Rangers. Colin likes the game to be exciting and fast. He takes a lot of knocks, as you see here, but he feels it's all part of a great game.

Let our attitude be that of the famous Mr. Alcock, who said away back in 1888:

'It is in the interests of football as well as the duty of those who govern it that the tone of the players should be maintained at the highest standard.

'The game to be played well must be played with a certain amount of spirit, and, indeed, without a modicum of excitement a great part of the charm would be gone. But its well-being depends entirely upon a common feeling of fair play and honest work and no penalty can be too severe for footballers who deviate from such a course, descending to tricks or devices with the object of getting a momentary advantage over an opponent, and evading the unwritten law of fairness which is essential to the maintenance of football as a national sport.'

Well said. We can't cry any more, 'Let there be hacking. . . .'

But we can still say, 'let there be excitement and action and fair physical contact.'

40

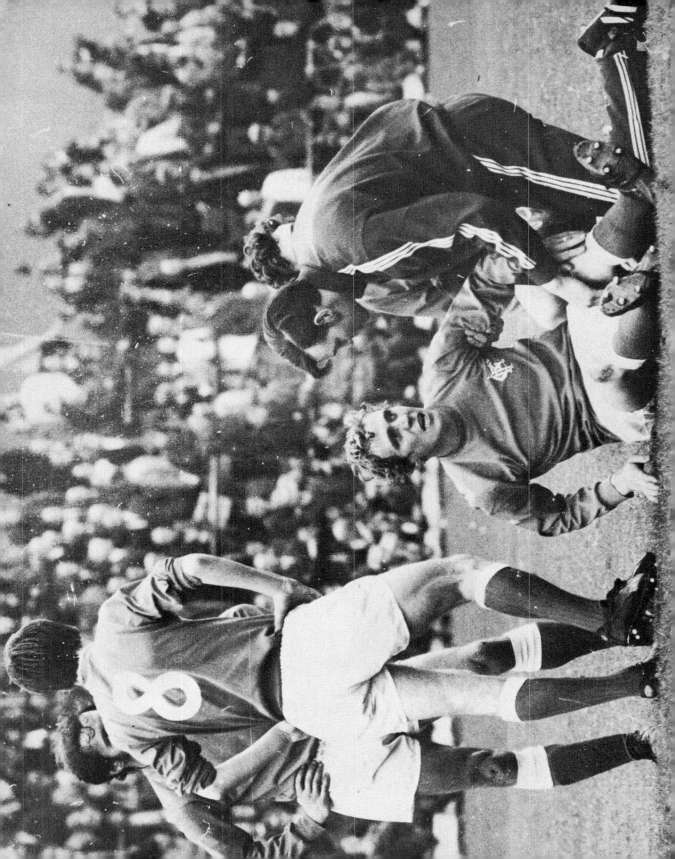

Who said football's not what it was? The blaze of excitement still keeps the crowd on the bawl

Football changes—but the arguments don't. They never will. After all, even in the old days, there were fans to complain that 'fitba's no' whit it was'. for there are always people who want things to stay as they are.

A row broke out, for instance, when Queen's Park, the soccer pioneers, decided the team should have a 'uniform'. The old-timers of the day didn't like that at all and they grumbled that the moderns were becoming too fussy.

What was wrong, they asked, with the different coloured cowls or night-caps, the head-dress affected by the pirate kings and smugglers of an earlier era, which distinguished the players, who all sported blue jerseys? (Incidentally, this is the reason Scotland wear blue shirts in internationals. Scotland wore these old blue guernseys in the first match against England in 1872 and we have stuck to that colour ever since.)

But changes had to come, despite the opposition and soon players were wearing club badges and, on the right arm, the distinguishing colour of the club.

And, in 1873, veteran Queen's Park members were sniffing, 'Players are becoming fops and dandies' when a new 'uniform' was introduced—red cap, blue jersey and white knickerbockers.

At that time, the players wore stockings of different colours, so that they could be identified by the spectators, just as jockeys are today.

Cards were issued by Queen's Park and would read like this: C. Campbell, red, white and black socks; Harry McNeill, orange and black; W. McKinnon, red; R.W. Neill, heather mixture—and T.C. Highet, black and white cap, no stockings . . . and so on.

Not everyone was satisfied, either, when the old rules, which allowed the ball to be fisted but not handled and condoned hacking, were changed.

Fierce arguments, too, arose over the evolution of the game. The English, who started football, relied on dribbling and made soccer an individual game. Queen's Park developed passing and their method of transference of the ball accompanied by strong backing up, got more out of a team. But many people thought that style was spoiling soccer.

And so it is today.

Many fans don't like the modern style and say method play is killing football.

But, say the advocates of the new football, method means more brain power, more intelligent play.

Nevertheless, one aspect of football never changes.

There are thrills galore in practically every game—and here's the proof. . . .

A selection of fine pictures which show why the crowds have always something to roar about.

42

Saved by a finger-tip . . . Dundee goalkeeper Ally Donaldson (now with Falkirk) survives a hectic moment as Rangers' Colin Stein goes up with him. The long arm—and finger-tip—of the 'keeper prevents a goal.

A flying tackle by Dundee's Bobby Wilson stops Celtic's Harry Hood breaking through in a sizzling moment at Parkhead.

Drama in the Kilmarnock goalmouth as goalkeeper Alistair Hunter, on the ground, nevertheless saves from Rangers' Graham Fyfe.

Morton 'keeper Erik Sorensen *(left)* **stretches desperately—but the crackling shot by Harry Hood, of Celtic, beats him.**

A grip like iron . . . an old phrase—but how better can you describe this sure clutch by Rangers' Peter McCloy *(above)*, **holding on grimly as he is challenged by Falkirk's Alex Ferguson.**

Near thing in the Airdrie goal-mouth *(left)*—but John Menzies is first to avert danger against Hibs with a life-saving header.

It's the mighty Derek Whiteford. This time the Airdrie skipper clears his lines in a clash with Hibernian.

Always in the Old Firm matches there's red-hot action. Here *(above)* you see Celtic's 'keeper, Evan Williams, getting down to a shot as Rangers' Colin Stein slides in.

And you can't say Stein isn't a persevering raider. He's on the spot again *(left)* as Hearts' Jim Cruickshanks blocks a shot from Colin Jackson.

Time marches on...

Time, an old phrase used to say, marches on. Not any more. Certainly not in football. In our great game, time *races* on.

There seems to be nothing more ephemeral than the life of a modern footballer. It's a sad thought—yet we can never forget the pleasure, the excitement and the drama the players provided for us, the onlookers.

That time flies by so rapidly was brought home to me when I looked back ten years to Scottish Football Book No. 8. I was writing: 'What a lot of changes there have been since the first Scottish Football Book was published. One of the articles was entitled "Up and Coming". It described some of Scotland's brightest young players of 1955–56. Alas, not all of them became household names.

'Two, John Davidson, of Falkirk, and George Brown, of Clyde, are no longer playing. At the end of the season, Tommy Gemmell, of St. Mirren, and Hugh Baird, of Airdrie, in 1956 regarded as two of our brightest prospects, were seeking new clubs.'

That was written in 1962, ten years ago. But—how much has the soccer scene changed since then?

In some ways, not much. Just as we do in 1972–73, we were hoping in 1962 that Scottish international football was starting a new era. We had at last just beaten England 2–0 at Hampden and had won by consummate skill. And we were sitting back complacent, believing we had a nucleus of young players who would quickly provide us with a team to compare with those of the golden years.

And we prided ourselves that we had stars of stars in the key positions—at wing-half and inside-forward. Crerand and Baxter . . . White and Law.

Well, that's what I mean by time flying.

We never did become a great power in international football. And that brilliant quartette can never now be the platform on which we can build a side to baffle Brazil. John White died tragically. Jim Baxter is out of football. Pat Crerand has his thoughts now on management. Only Denis Law continues to play with the power and the glory that made him one of soccer's immortals.

So much for high hopes. These players had the skill and the know-how and the temperament to make Scotland really great. Why didn't they? One reason was that, as always, it seemed impossible for the S.F.A. to field them all at the same time in internationals. Because of injuries, club commitments?

That counted. But it seems to me that one of the principal reasons for our decline in international football is that we do not try hard enough to make our team selection a continuing story. Indeed, it is just about ten years ago, in Madrid in the early summer of 1963,

But the past, thank goodness, is still with us

that Scotland recorded her best result in modern times, a 6–2 win over Spain—and also played superlative football, football even the South Americans would have envied.

What happened? That wonderful team never played together again—no, not once. Don't tell me these stars couldn't have turned out again.

Let's hope that under the bright new managership of Tommy Docherty the old, sorry chop-and-change policy disappears.

It was on April 28, 1962, that Dundee beat St. Johnstone 3–0 at Muirton, won the League Championship for the first time in their 70 years' history—and,

incidentally, put Saints into the Second Division on goal average.

What a triumph it was for the Dens Park men. For years they had been Scotland's mystery team. Always noted for entertainment, blessed with a succession of bonnie elevens, Dundee had, alas, all too often lacked the killer touch.

But in 1962 Dundee were at last putting the ball into the net regularly. What was their secret? At a time when method was creeping in and many Scottish team formations appeared to be something of a "vital statistics" report, what with 4–2–4, 3–3–4 and other amazing permutations, Dundee had only one gimmick—good football.

The words of their manager, Bob Shankly, now with Stirling Albion, were wise then—and wise today. Said Bob of his title triumph: 'You must play football as you see fit. When a side takes the field it can have as many plans and Continental ideas as it wants but for the 90 minutes the team can only play as well as the opposition can allow. The players must be intelligent enough to read the game as it goes on.'

Bob Shankly and his men struck a great blow for good old-fashioned Scottish football at a time when it appeared that other clubs should have been employing a mathematician instead of a manager.

Dundee used what I called then 'a half-lob'. This was used with devastating effect by brilliant ball artists like Gordon Smith and Andy Penman. They controlled their passes so beautifully that crackshots like Alan Gilzean and Alan Cousin could run ON to the ball and be in perfect balance as well as perfect position when they shot.

What a contrast all this was to other teams whose passes came at such speed that the players for whom they were intended had to worry more about getting the ball under control than about being in position when shooting.

Old-fashioned? Perhaps. But the lessons of Dundee should be heeded in 1972-73. They can still win honours.

Ian McMillan doesn't look too happy in this picture. It's a cold, wet day and the team he manages, Airdrie, aren't doing too well. But every time one of the older fans looks at Ian he sees ... joy, artistry, the velvet touch. For McMillan was one of the greatest of all-time inside-forwards, the players who were the pride and joy of Scotland.

Hibs have always been noted for famous centre-forwards. And in the last decade Joe Baker, smiling here, was a terrific leader. Joe took over the mantle of the lethal Lawrie Reilly. Now—who will follow in Joe's famous footsteps at Easter Road?

Superb artist—that was Gordon Smith, perhaps the most elegant right winger of all time. Gordon's retired now and, let's be frank, there are few today who can remind us of the Gay Hib. He was in a class of his own.

After all, Dundee became more methodical—and have never won the title again.

Balance, skill, experience, old-style know-how—Dundee had all that. When they get it again, they'll be really challenging for another title.

Who were the players of the moment in 1962? The men the fans loved included John Cumming, of Hearts, Alastair McLeod, of Hibernian, and Harry Melrose, of Dunfermline Athletic.

Dedicated players all—and players who are still in the game, playing vital roles for clubs as managers and trainers. Alas, there were others making the crowds roar ten years ago who appear to have vanished from the soccer scene. Remember them? Remember Peter Price, of Ayr United and Raith Rovers, a centre-forward in the old-style? Remember Bertie Black, of Kilmarnock, a cultured inside-forward with the velvet touch? Remember Bobby Carroll, of Celtic, a former Irvine Meadow winger who was reckoned the snappiest the junior grade had ever turned out.

Yes, time flies on, the actors depart the stage.

But there's a bright side. Always coming on are bright young men, invariably helped and inspired by those who went before them.

Just as Billy Steel undoubtedly wanted to emulate Bob McPhail, just as Lawrie Reilly determined to be a new Hughie Gallacher, just as Joe Baker wanted to mould himself on Lawrie Reilly, just as Jim Brown tries to find the touch of Davie McKay in his play, for Hearts, so does Kenny Dalglish hope to be a new Bobby Murdoch, Iain MacDonald a new Davy Wilson and Arthur Duncan a modern Willie Ormond.

So it's consolation to know that the past we loved is still with us, really, in much of the style of the players of today.

Who can ever forget them—Law and Baxter? What a pair, what brilliance, what excitement they produced. Alas, Jim Baxter is out of football—but Denis plays on, as fiery as ever. Here you see them, ecstatic, after one of the greatest moments in Scottish football history, defeat of England at Wembley.

THISTLE SIZZLE

Thistle's goal-scorers with the League Cup—Alex Rae, Jimmy Bone, Denis McQuade and Bobby Lawrie.

. . . and win the League Cup

October 23, 1971, is probably the most important date in the history of Partick Thistle. Not only is it the date of their greatest triumph; it is the date which marked a new era for the Jags of Maryhill.

Until that memorable Saturday after-

57

noon, Thistle had been known as the Old Unpredictables. Everybody in football liked them for they invariably provided the unexpected: thrills, laced with comedy; triumph, followed by tragedy. Excitement, drama—and fun: these went hand in hand at Firhill. Thistle folk all had the same rather happy-go-lucky spirit, invariably optimistic about their team but never drearily upset to the point of wife-beating if the Jags lost.

Even their one tremendous triumph, a Scottish Cup victory in the final of 1921, could only have been achieved by the rollicking men of Firhill; for it was a victory that contained everything from near disaster to Charlie Chaplin comedy.

For instance, to reach the final they played four ties—but, because of replays, it took them TEN desperate games before they met Rangers in the final. Then there was a row about the Cup Final venue. Celtic Park was chosen but only 28,000 spectators turned up—because the admission charge had been increased to two shillings.

Thistle had team worries and they were so badly hit by injury that Jimmy McMenemy, the former Celtic star who had become the Jags' coach, had to take the field.

But Thistle won—because Rangers' Jimmy Bowie had to leave the pitch to don a new pair of pants, his own having been torn. And when he was off, John Blair scored. And that goal won the cup for Thistle.

Skipper Alex Rae scores Thistle's first goal.

A fine win—but it caused a lot of laughs. And that was the Thistle story right down the years.

Until October 23, 1971.

Not everyone at Firhill was happy about the Thistle image—especially new manager David McParland, one of the all-time Firhill favourites as a player.

With a dedicated staff, one of whom was Scot Symon, a former Rangers manager, and enthusiastic players, manager McParland gave Firhill a new look and a new spirit. And although Partick Thistle had newly gained promotion from the Second Division only at the end of the previous season they quickly had the music hall comics looking for new gags for the team had suddenly become predictable—playing fast, solid, attractive football.

Incredibly, it seemed, Thistle found themselves only a game away from their first top honour in 50 years—deservedly into the final of the League Cup.

But few football fans outwith the old grey tenements of Maryhill gave even the new, inspired Thistle much chance.

For they had to face Celtic—and Celtic, who had lost the final the year before to Rangers, were determined that they would be successful in their amazing eight-finals-in-a-row bid.

The bookmakers had no doubts. They had Celtic at four to one on.

And between the clubs seemed to be all the difference in the fascinating world of soccer.

Harry Hood illustrates Celtic's determination to hit back as he dives for a cross in the Thistle goal area.

Thistle had just emerged from a spell in which they played before a few hundred spectators at places such as Brechin, Forfar and Stranraer.

Celtic were among the greatest clubs in the world. It had just been proved by mathematical percentages that they had the best club record of all in the European Cup-winners Cup, though they had never won it, and were rated fourth in the all-time European Cup charts with a percentage rating of 67.19 from the 32 ties they had played to that date.

But Thistle feared no-one. After all, they had already in a fabulous start to the season beaten Rangers, Falkirk and St. Johnstone.

This was how the finalists had won through to Hampden:
Celtic—In Section Five, they beat Rangers 2–0 and 3–0, beat Morton 1–0 away but lost 0–1 at Parkhead, beat Ayr United 3–0 and 4–1; in the quarter-final, they beat Clydebank 5–0 and 6–2; and, in the semi-final, they beat St. Mirren 3–0 at Hampden, scoring 27 goals and losing 4.
Thistle—In Section Seven, they beat Arbroath 4–0 and 4–2, beat East Fife 3–2 away and drew with them 1–1 at Firhill, drew 1–1 with Raith Rovers away and beat them 5–0 at home. In the supplementary play-off, they beat Alloa 4–1 at home and drew 1–1 away; in the quarter-final, they lost to St. Johnstone 0–2 away and won 5–1 at home; and, in the semi–final, they beat Falkirk 2–0 at Hampden, scoring 30 goals and losing 11.

The stage was set for a game in which all the spectacular skills of Scottish football at its best would be on display—a clash of opposites, yet opposites who had much in common.

What they had in common was an enthusiasm for all-out attacking football.

But no-one knew just how dramatic this League Final of 1971 was going to be.

A crowd of 62,740 turned up at Hampden on October 23.

Celtic were without skipper Billy McNeill, who had been enjoying a fine season but who was a victim of muscle strain, and Bobby Murdoch was the captain for the big day. Skipper of Thistle was inside-forward Alex Rae, former Bury and East Fife player.

The line-up was:
Celtic—Williams, Hay, Gemmell, Murdoch, Connelly, Brogan, Johnstone, Dalglish, Hood, Callaghan, Macari. Sub—Craig.
Thistle—Rough, Hansen, Forsyth, Glavin, Campbell, Strachan, McQuade, Coulston, Bone, Rae, Lawrie. Sub—Gibson.
Referee—W. J. Mullan, Dalkeith.

Thistle fans were hoping that through the game there would be a golden thread—the thread of glittering wing play that had helped their team to glory.

They didn't realise that long before the end of the game they would be voiceless.

There has never been a more sensational first half at Hampden. And Celtic, veteran campaigners in the white heat of Europe, never knew what hit them.

Brash but confident, Thistle went swinging into the attack right from the whistle. And the neutrals were saying they hoped Thistle would score an early goal so that it might be a real game, with Celtic having something to fight for.

The truth was that Thistle played the kind of fast, exciting football that used to be a Celtic copyright. Strangely, Celtic played studied soccer, seemingly content

60

Celtic's Evan Williams gets to the ball a second before all-action Jimmy Bone, Thistle striker.

Jimmy Bone scores Thistle's fourth goal as the Celtic defence stand like statues.

to try to gain control of the middle. This was mistaken strategy—for Thistle had only one interest, to shoot into the Celtic penalty area with all speed and fire possible.

And suddenly Thistle's sensationally bright play made us all forget overcast and dreary Hampden on a dull October afternoon.

Their wingers were worrying a Celtic defence that missed the generalship of McNeill and in the ninth minute they went ahead with a memorable goal.

After Bone and McQuade had earned cheers with respectable shots, Thistle won a corner, thanks mainly to sloppy defensive work by the Celts. And the rearguard were still sloppy when the ball came over. It went to the foot of Rae on the edge of the penalty area and, with a lunge of his lethal right foot, the Thistle skipper thundered the ball into the top of the net.

As the Maryhill fans went wild, Celtic supporters consoled themselves with the thought that this must be a fluke. These thoughts didn't remain long with them.

Instead of surging forward, their pride hurt, and eager to show the upstart Thistle what football was about, Celtic seemed paralysed—and soon they were pulverised. For the goal spurred Thistle's eager youngsters to even greater endeavour.

Celtic failed to take command in the middle, where the strong-tackling Glavin and Rae were proving a powerful partnership, breaking up the Celtic attacks and finding time to drum on their own attackers.

Celtic looked the outsiders, not Partick.

And in the 15th minute Thistle struck again.

It was a goal which showed that had any doubt about the reality and danger

of the Thistle challenge existed it had vanished speedily.

Thistle were sizzling and deft winger Bobby Lawrie took a perfect pass from Bone, beat Hay on the left, cut in, changed feet at the critical moment and sent a brilliant shot into the far corner of the net.

Now Celtic were in real trouble and to add to their difficulties Jimmy Johnstone, the dazzling winger on whom they had pinned their hopes, had to go off in the 17th minute with a leg injury. Hay moved to midfield to accommodate substitute Craig at full-back.

But this was Thistle's day. They kept

up their hot attacks, preventing Celtic from moving into their usual rhythm. Using the wings to devastating effect, they mercilessly stretched a Celtic defence which grew more nervous with every fierce raid.

Celtic fans couldn't believe it—and worse was to come. A Lawrie corner kick in the 30th minute again caught the Celtic defence at panic stations and in the scrimmage in front of goal when the ball came over lanky Denis McQuade simply toe-ended the ball into the net.

Never had Celtic been so embarrassed. No-one could remember when they had been three down to another Scottish side. No-one could remember when they had been so badly outplayed, their forwards harmless, their mid-field men striving frantically but ineffectively, and their defence in a dreadful tangle against the pace and skills of wingers McQuade and Lawrie and the magnificent double striking partnership of Bone and Coulston.

Worse was to come for the Celts. Incredibly, in the 36th minute, Bone was allowed all the time and room in the world to saunter forward after Lawrie had taken a free kick and prod the ball into the net, with Celtic defenders looking on, like men caught in a quicksand.

At half-time it was 4–0 for Thistle—and still few could believe it. Across the city at Ibrox, Rangers, playing Motherwell, had been booed off the field by their own fans. Then the Hampden result was announced over the loud-speakers. The Rangers fans set up the loudest cheer of the season—and urged on their own players to a 4–0 win.

But Celtic are a proud team—and a good team. They recovered from their ills and pushed up the pace to such an extent that some of their attacking was awesome.

They improved enormously in the second half, making chances regularly and brilliantly—but they could not find their scoring touch.

A Murdoch shot thumped into the side netting. Dalglish took the ball through—but chipped it over the bar. Another flick from the aggressive forward struck Rough's body and went for a corner. And now Alan Rough, that up-and-coming goalkeeper, was inspired, saving a Macari shot at point-blank range.

At last Celtic's football was the football of old, magnificent in its method, pace and inventiveness. At last, too, Thistle wilted but they held on, thanks to the inspiring Rough.

With 20 minutes left, Dalglish scored for Celtic but by then it didn't matter.

Thistle still had moves and they brought on young Gibson for the limping Glavin and this bright winger showed commendable touches.

In the end, there was no doubt about Thistle's 4–1 victory. They had beaten Celtic at their own game and while it was true that the Celtic defence showed moments of shocking and unusual incompetence the credit goes to Thistle who put their opponents under alarming pressure by their speed and flair.

And what a night it was in old Maryhill, as the giant-killers were toasted by thousands of jubilant supporters. Traffic was halted as the trophy —bedecked with Thistle's red and yellow colours—was borne back to Firhill. Fans hung from tenement windows, shouting congratulations.

It was a richly-earned success for the young Jags—and it was also a wonderful League Cup Final, with Celtic hitting back in the fine second half.

Happy Thistle and chairman Jimmy Aitken, also President of the Scottish League, celebrate their win.

It's the superior Soccer Quiz that separates the men from the boys

It's time for a cheer—or a groan. Depends, you see, on just how keen a football enthusiast you are, a man who can hold his own with the best referee, learned historian or clever soccer Dick—or just a fan who bawls 'Getin-taethem'.

For it's our famous superior football quiz again, the quiz you either love or hate . . . but the quiz, nevertheless, that proves whether or not you're a real expert.

Here we go, then.

With, as always, an easy start . . . perhaps.

1.—A mixed bag. (a) When were goal nets invented? (b) Which was the first Scottish club outside Glasgow and Edinburgh to play in the European Cup? (c) What player scored five goals for Scotland in an international match? (d) Are corner flags optional or compulsory? (e) When should a referee allow play to continue even though a foul has been committed?

2.—Puzzle Corner. What club? To get the right club, insert its name between the two lines of letters below. If you pick the right Scottish club, you will have ten 3-letter words reading downwards.

S O A I P F I D I E
— — — — — — — — — —
I L L P L Y K T E E

Noughts and Crosses. Instead of the noughts and crosses listed below, make six-letter words which fit the clues. If you're right, you'll find that the diagonal line of nought is replaced by the name of a Scottish League club.

OXXXXX Aberdeen player
XOXXXX English internationalist
XXOXXX A goal can be scored with this
XXXOXX A Wolf who strikes
XXXXOX What a centre-forward does
XXXXXO Football clubs—or dogs?

3.—Fancy yourself as a referee? Well, what would you do in the following cases?

(a) The winger is about to take a corner kick—but he places the ball OUTSIDE the permitted arc. As the referee, do you come over and replace the ball inside the arc—or do you allow the player to take the corner and then penalise him for an infringement?

(b) It's just on half-time. Rangers are awarded a penalty kick. To the cheers of the home fans, United's keeper makes a great save. But the ball rebounds to the Rangers' penalty-taker, who shoots it into the net. Do you give a goal?

(c) In a hectic cup-tie, McGregor of Athletic and Lawrie of Wanderers rush to the ball. Both get to it at the same time. Both get a foot to it simultaneously. The ball skids out of play. What's your decision?

4.—Now for the quickies. (a) Are Celtic an older club than Rangers? (b) Have Airdrie ever won the Scottish Cup? (c) Who is Dundee's most capped player? (d) From which countries do the following clubs come: Ferencvaros, Servette, Galatasaray, Feyenoord, Varese, Vojvodina? (e) Which team scored most goals in a Scottish Cup-tie? (f) When does a game actually start? (g) In a League match, which team kicks off at the beginning of extra time?

5.—The date-line is—Hampden 1929. Now, who is the 'reporter' who wrote the following story, entitled 'Was it a Goal?'

'The arguments are still raging at Hampden this breezy afternoon as the 110,500 spectators leave after one of football's most sensational incidents.

'This is what the crowd saw:

'It's the last minute of the Scotland England international. Scotland, who lost right-winger Alec Jackson just before half-time, force a corner.

'I have been playing inside-right but, with Jackson out of action, I take the kick.

'I try to judge the wind.'

Well, who am I?

'Say my colleagues in the Scottish side:

"Of course, it was a goal. The flight of the ball deceived Hacking."

'Say the English players: "It wasn't a goal. Hacking was impeded. It should have been a foul."

'The arguments will rage for a long, long time—but the goal stands.'

Well, who took that corner kick?

6.—If you think you're really the tops so far . . . just try your luck with these tough ones.

(a) All are famous clubs—but can you recognise them from these former titles . . . . Wee Alpha, Orion, Excelsior, Small Heath Alliance, Newton Heath, Christ Church Sunday School, Thames Ironworks?

(b) What started the Hampden Riot in 1909? And when was the first Ibrox disaster?

(c) It's said that Hungary were the first foreign team to defeat England on their own soil by 6–3 at Wembley in 1953? Is this true?

7.—OK, so you're good. How about ending on a high note? Can you name the grounds at which these pictures were taken?
A
B
C
D
E
F

Answers on pages 71, 72.

F

Quiz answers

1.—Mixed bag. (a) In 1890 by J. A. Brodie, of Liverpool. (b) Dundee (c) Hughie Gallacher (d) Compulsory (e) When he feels that to stop the game for a free kick would give the offending side an advantage.

2.—What club?
S O A I P F I D I E
K I L M A R N O C K
I L L P L Y K T E E

Noughts and crosses
Harper
Peters
He**a**der
Cu**r**ran
Shoots
Rover**s**   Club:—Hearts

3.—You're the ref. (a) In Scotland, the S.F.A. tell referees not to interfere and if the player takes a corner outside the arc an indirect free kick should be given. In other countries, however, the referee is instructed to make sure the player places the ball inside the arc before taking the kick.
(b) No. You must blow for the end of the first half as soon as the penalty kick is saved if you are satisfied it is exactly on half-time when the keeper handles.
(c) You drop the ball where it was last played.

4.—Quickies. (a) No, Celtic were formed in 1888, Rangers in 1873. (b) Yes, in 1924. (c) Alec Hamilton, with 24 full caps. (d) Ferencvaros—Hungary, Servette—Switzerland, Galatasaray —Turkey, Feyenoord—Holland, Varese—Italy, Vojvodina—Yugoslavia. (e) Arbroath in beating Bon Accord 36–0 in 1885. (f) Tricky one for the rule says, 'The referee having given a signal, the game shall be started by a player kicking the ball into his opponents' half of the field'—but my interpretation is that the game only starts when the player kicks the ball . . . after all, football's about kicking the ball, isn't it? (g) Neither—extra time isn't played in a Scottish League match.

5.—The 'reporter' is Alex Cheyne, of Aberdeen.
6.—(a) Wee Alpha—Motherwell, Orion—Aberdeen, Excelsior—Airdrie, Small Heath Alliance—Birmingham, Newton Heath—Manchester United, Christ Church Sunday School—Bolton Wanderers, Thames Ironworks—West Ham United.
(b) The Hampden Riot was due to a misunderstanding about the playing of extra time at the end of the Rangers – Celtic Cup Final in 1909. The field was invaded by angry spectators who uprooted goalposts, corner and touchline flags and then set fire to anything they could lay their hands on. Sequel was that the Cup was withheld. Queen's Park claimed damages and received £500 from the S.F.A. and £150 from both Celtic and Rangers. The Ibrox disaster occured in 1902 when the timber terracing collapsed and 25 spectators lost their lives and around 500 were injured.
(c) If you consider Eire a foreign team, they take the honour of being the first country to beat England on their own soil. They triumphed 2–0 over England at Goodison Park, Liverpool, in 1949.

7.—A is Fir Park, Motherwell—and it's a
    match with Dundee.
    B is Bayview Park, Methil—and Dave Gorman, the East Fife goalkeeper, makes a save during a match with Rangers.
    C is Somerset Park, Ayr, and Celtic have just scored against Ayr United.
    D is Broomfield Park, Airdrie, and Arthur Duncan, of Hibs, is scoring.
    E is Firhill—and it's Partick Thistle v Dunfermline.
    F is a tricky one—for this is Windsor Park, Belfast, and Scotland, as you can see, are overjoyed after scoring against Ireland in an international.

72

DO YOU KNOW THAT . . .

. . . ARBROATH are the oldest football club north of the Forth? They were formed in 1878 and have always been noted for their fighting qualities.

Certainly Rangers know that. There was nothing Arbroath liked better in the old days than to upset the crack teams from the West. And there was a sensation when they faced Rangers in a Scottish Cup-tie at Gayfield in 1884. Arbroath won 2–1.

At once Rangers protested bitterly. They complained about the size of the ground and, indeed, sent back to Glasgow a wire message which said:

'Beaten on a back green.'

The appeal was dismissed. Again Rangers appealed. This time it was upheld and the tie was ordered to be replayed. This time, too, the ground was extended by three feet—and Rangers won the replay.

Hearts are one of our greatest old clubs—and Jim Cruikshanks, their goalkeeper, is one of the best in his position in Scotland.

Arbroath, however, have a record which is unlikely ever to be shattered. In a Scottish Cup-tie two years after their game with Rangers, they created the senior record score, beating Bon-Accord of Aberdeen by 36–0. That was in 1886.

Before they stepped up to the Second Division, Arbroath had been pioneers in the Northern and Central Leagues and have had their name inscribed on the Scottish Qualifying Cup when that trophy was regarded as the real blue riband of provincial football in Scotland.

. . . EAST FIFE are probably the most renowned cup-fighters of all the provincial clubs in Scotland?

Founded in 1903, they became the talk of Scottish football in season 1926–27. Although still in the Second Division, they played so well in the Scottish Cup that they reached the final. They faced Celtic and it was their bad luck that that was the season in which Jimmy McGrory was in rampant mood. By February, McGrory had beaten the record League aggregate of 45 goals scored in one season.

Celtic had qualified for the final for the 19th time and the Fifers were Hampden newcomers. But the men from Methil put up a magnificent show before going down 3–1 to the Glasgow crack-shots.

But East Fife had the taste for the big-time and in 1929–30 they gained promotion.

They were soon back in the Second Division, alas, but still they found fame in the Scottish Cup. And in 1938 they brought fame to the lower league—for they won the Scottish Cup.

They had been real dark horses, beating Aberdeen but taking three games in the semi-final against St. Bernards before marching through to the final to face First Division Kilmarnock.

Killie had knocked out both Rangers and Celtic in previous rounds and were hot favourites to take the trophy. But East Fife showed their cup prowess and drew the first match—a 1–1 draw. A crowd of 92,000 saw the replay which proved a thriller.

East Fife were immense, especially in extra time. McKerrell opened the scoring for the Fifers. Then Kilmarnock got on top, but the 90 minutes ended 2–2. In extra time, McKerrell and Miller got the goals which gave East Fife a 4–2 victory.

The history-making Fife side was: Milton, Laird, Tait, Russell, Sneddon, Harvey, Adams, McLeod, McCartney, Miller, McKerrell. John Harvey, later to become Hearts manager, took over from Herd, who had been injured in the first game of the final.

. . . HEART OF MIDLOTHIAN fans still argue about how the famous Edinburgh club, formed in 1873, received its name?

Some say it came from—a dance hall! The Heart of Midlothian was a palais off the Royal Mile and, so the story goes, youths who frequented it once joked with a policeman at the Tron Kirk around New Year time. The policeman told them they would be better employed kicking a ball about in the Meadows than dancing. So a band of the lads clubbed together and bought a ball, so forming the football club and naming it after their favourite dance hall.

Others are of the opinion that the club originated with lads who played football in the street around the site of the old Edinburgh Tolbooth near St. Giles'

East Fife didn't make much of a hit in last season's Scottish Cup. But in goalkeeper Dave Gorman, seen here in action at Bayview, they have a top star of today—and a player who has all the determination of the great Methil cup-fighters of the past.

Kilmarnock's floodlights are much brighter now than they were when the first game by "electric light" was played at Rugby Park last century. In this modern picture, Killie's Jackie McGrory goes after Colin Stein, of Rangers.

Motherwell heroes of today are hardly in the elegant tradition of their famous left-wing, Stevenson and Ferrier. But they still play with a verve which worries the Old Firm. The new Motherwell outlook, all for one and one for all, is seen here *(left)* as Watson, Forsyth and McCallum try to stop Rangers' Derek Johnstone in a game at Fir Park.

Cathedral. This was the jail known as the Heart of Midlothian and pulled down early in the 19th century.

There seems no doubt, though, that directly or indirectly the Hearts took their name from the old jail, with Sir Walter Scott's novel, The Heart of Midlothian, keeping the grim old dungeon fresh in mind.

Hearts began their career at the Meadows, a public park. Then they moved to Powderhall. And in 1881 Hearts switched to the Tynecastle district.

In the First War, Hearts supplied the

nucleus of a whole battalion of the Royal Scots, and many of the players laid down their lives.

. . . KILMARNOCK are the pioneers of floodlight football—and organised the first game under artificial light as far back as 1878?

The game between Kilmarnock and local rivals, Portland, took place at Rugby Park on November 8 of that year and attracted 'an immense number of people to see the novel game'.

Lighting was supplied by E. Paterson, a London electrical engineer. There were three lamps, 'the motive power of which was provided by a traction and two portable engines of six and eight horse power', according to an old report of the game.

Compared with modern installations which turn night into day, the lights were primitive. At one end of the field was one large light, affording an illumination of 6,000 candles and, at the opposite corners, one light each, with an illumination of 12,000 candles. The lights were generated from three Siemen's electric 'gynamos'—the name then for a dynamo.

The Kilmarnock historian said: 'The field was illuminated with an intensely brilliant and, at the same time, beautifully soft radiance.' But apparently there was a want of diffusion so that between the rays there were intervals of deep shadow, in which it was difficult to follow play.

Although the experiment was hailed as a success, it wasn't repeated. For play proved dangerous in the flickering light—and two Kilmarnock stars, Baillie Miller and J. B. Wilson, were so seriously injured that they never played again.

Kilmarnock are now the second oldest of the Scottish clubs, having been formed in 1869, two years after the birth of Queen's Park.

For Third Lanark, founded in 1868, are, of course, no longer with us.

. . . MOTHERWELL had the greatest wing pair football has ever known—George Stevenson and Bobby Ferrier?

Times have changed and football in the 1970's is more resolute, more mathematical, perhaps, but I still feel that the old Scottish wing play was magnificent to watch, real artistry, poetry in motion. And I have no doubt that if players with the talent of Stevenson and Ferrier were around today they could revive the most entrancing of all football arts, wing combination.

The partnership of Stevenson and Ferrier began in 1923–24 and they were as famous abroad as they were at Fir Park. In South Africa, where Motherwell's elegant play was so populai, schoolboys came in crowds, mainly to study the play of the great wing pair.

Ferrier of the deadly left foot joined Motherwell from Petershill and only the accident of his birth—he was born in Sheffield—prevented him from gaining top international honours. He played, however, for the Scottish League.

Stevenson was a product of Kilbirnie Ladeside and won many caps.

But they were twins in thought, if not in action, and I have never seen a more effective partnership.

Motherwell, formed in 1885, are one of the classic sides and in season 1931–32 they made history by breaking the Old Firm monopoly to win the Scottish League championship.

Oh! The agony of it all

Football is a game of high drama, emotion, passion. And footballers can be as temperamental as actors. Not for our soccer heroes the grim mask of stoicism, the unaltered expression, when fortunes rise—or fall.

No, indeed.

They greet a goal with all the joy of a Hollywood star, cast as the victim of the Apaches, listening to the approach of the 7th Cavalry.

They roll in agony when they're fouled with all the frenzy of a rival gangster caught in a hail of Al Capone bullets.

Sometimes you think they should be given Oscars instead of Golden Boots for their performances.

Let's face it, though. The fans love it all. Football has a touch of show business nowadays.

So meet some of our star-studded cast in moments of emotion—mainly agony—during the season.

This time it's the turn of Partick Thistle's Hugh Strachan to show all the despair of a man who has caused an atomic disaster. The Firhill defender has turned the ball into his own net—in a match against Celtic.

Oh, God, what have I done, what have I done. Say it isn't true. Say it's just a nightmare. Alas, it's all too true. And Celtic skipper Billy McNeill wishes he could bury himself in the ground after scoring against his own side in a vital match with Aberdeen. The Greek chorus of woe is provided by his colleagues, Denis Connaghan and Jim Brogan, while Aberdeen's Steve Murray takes the good news back to his mates.

Expression grim, teeth clenched, lines of worry around his eyes,
George Miller shows all the agony of a manager whose team fights
to avoid relegation. George had just been appointed manager of
Dunfermline Athletic when this picture was taken. He sits beside
trainer Andy Stevenson at Parkhead—and sees his club beaten by
the only goal of the game.

81

Ouch, that was sore! But determination is mixed with agony as
Motherwell's leader, Jim McCabe, and Rangers' goalkeeper Peter
McCloy go for a cross in a match at Fir Park.

The net hides the expression on the face of Peter McCloy in this picture. But you can guess at just how the big keeper looks as he fishes the ball from the back of the net. Who said—agonised?

And what about this for a spectrum of all the soccer emotions? Hibs hail a last-minute goal at Parkhead. But Celtic players plead frantically that the scorer was off-side. It's a field day for a film producer looking for actors. In the end, the goal was disallowed.

Death or Glory Boys

in action

Covered in mud. Cold. More often jeered than cheered. Called on to perform prodigies of heroism. But classed not by the great saves they make but by their mistakes.

The goalkeepers. The men who stand alone. The fall guys.

No-one can deny that the goalkeepers are the death or glory boys of football or that they are the bravest of the brave, diving desperately at the feet of forwards, clutching swirling centres as strikers whizz in on them like rockets and stopping thundering shots at point-blank range.

Yet they are remembered far more for an error than for a brilliant save.

Who'd be a goalkeeper?

Amazingly, hundreds of Scottish youngsters still fancy themselves as new Jimmy Cowans, John Thomsons or Jerry Dawsons.

Which is a contrast to the situation in Brazil, the home of the world champions.

There no-one wants to be a keeper. All the kids clamour to be Pele, Tostao, Jairzinho. In the thousands of kick-arounds on the sands of Rio or the well-kept pitches in the country, there are tears and petulant stamps when a kid is asked to play in goal. Everyone wants to be an outfield player, trying to emulate the skills and artistry of the country's football kings.

Perhaps the pitches have something to do with the fact that this country still produces the great keepers while the South Americans are invariably worried about that key position.

In Brazil, for example, the sands make soccer pitches as well prepared as a wicket at Lords. In Scotland, pitches are all too often muddy, riddled with mounds and divots, dotted with more ridges than the Grampians.

In Brazil, the kids love to show off on perfect surfaces. Here, lads give up outfield play in disgust and begin to express themselves in goal where the ground doesn't matter so much.

Keepers are the unsung heroes, however. Why do they do it?

After all, a miss by a forward is soon forgotten—but if the keeper drops a cross and lets one in he's in trouble with the fans for the rest of the game . . . and maybe the rest of the season.

And keepers are undervalued soccer citizens in comparison with the other players. For instance, the record British transfer fee (at the time of writing, that is, for the money goes up so swiftly these

Fearlessly, Hearts goalkeeper Jim Cruikshanks dives at the feet of Bobby Lennox, of Celtic. It's all in the day's work for the 'keeper, to whom valour is merely a built-in attribute.

Nowadays goalies are becoming more colourful. Jim Herriot, of Hibernian, favours a flowing hair style—but it doesn't hinder his agility and here he moves in quickly to thwart Billy McNeill, of Celtic.

days) is £220,000, paid by Arsenal to Everton for Alan Ball. Yet the highest fee paid for a goalkeeper is £65,000 by West Ham for Bobby Ferguson—and that was way back in 1967.

And the tension for a keeper is unbelievable. Football's a team game—but keepers are usually called on to act alone—and they are most often the men who hold their team's fate in their hands.

Why, I repeat, do they do it?

For one thing, keepers are usually flamboyant characters. They like to be in the limelight. There's a touch of eccentricity about the best of them. It's said you don't have to be daft to be a goalkeeper—but it helps.

It has also been said that small boys who have large egos like to be goalkeepers because they can kick the ball further than anyone else and order their pals about.

There is also the fact that goalkeepers last longer than most. As Abraham Lincoln said, "It is better to adhere to the old and the tried than to trust the new and the untried." And great goalkeepers seem to go on for ever. There was Frank Swift, Alf Wood, Ted Sagar, Ronnie Simpson. Undoubtedly the most dubious privilege in our great game is to be the deputy to one of the truly princely keepers . . . they go on for ever and ever.

It was Jimmy Brown, though, who best described the reasons why a youngster wants to go into goal. And Jimmy should know, having been one of this country's most brilliant, colourful and acrobatic goalkeepers with Hearts, Kilmarnock and St. Mirren.

Said the bold James: 'A goalkeeper has to be everything. He has to have mathematical, meteorological and psychological learning. For he must be able to bisect angles so as to perplex some

Well clutched! Ally Donaldson, of Falkirk, firmly holds a shot during a match against Rangers.

It's not all glory being a 'keeper. Peter McCloy of Rangers knows that as he moves the wrong way to try to save a penalty taken by Kenny Dalglish, of Celtic.

Goalkeeping, of course, isn't all leaping, diving, slithering, punching, clutching. You're not a hero all the time—or a villain. Sometimes you're a director. And here Airdrie's Roddy McKenzie gives instructions to his fellow defenders as they line up at a free kick.

What's this, a 'keeper having a passing game with an opponent? Not on your life. Erik Sorensen, of Morton, is one of the best 'keepers in the land and he stops a shot at point-blank range from Celtic's Bobby Lennox with his leg—an instinctive save.

eager forward or to deflect rising balls over the bar. He must be able to sense what effect wind or rain may have on a corner kick or a high cross. And he must be a bit of a psychologist by sensing the probable direction of shots.

That goalkeeping can be dangerous is proved by the tragic case of John Thomson, of Celtic, who was killed in a match against Rangers.

John was 18 when he was signed from Wellesley Juniors and, as the Celtic chronicler says, 'the generation that saw Thomson in action will agree that it would be hard to exaggerate his magical skill and the same generation will acknowledge that neither before nor since have they seen a goalkeeper so swift, so elegant, so superbly safe in operation. He had the spring of a jaguar and the effortless grace of a skimming swallow. To see him Saturday after Saturday moving lithely between his posts gave to the fortunate onlookers the same intensity of satisfaction that plays and the opera, lift of romance and the high, vibrant pitch of great verse convey to minds more interested in things of the spirit.'

Once again Scotland is rich in goalkeepers. For a spell we wondered what had happened to the current crop for there seemed no-one to assume the mantle of Thomson, Dawson, Cowan, Jackson, Harper or Harkness. But you can't keep good goalies down and now claims for places in our international team are being staked by Bobby Clark, of Aberdeen, Alistair Hunter, of Kilmarnock, Alan Rough, of Partick Thistle, Mike Hewitt, of Dundee, and Keith McCrae, of Motherwell.

Back to top form is Motherwell's Keith McCrae, one of the outstanding young 'keepers in Scotland.

92

One of the myths about football is that only the so-called 'lower classes' understand and support the game. As far back as 1909, *The Times*, that explosive organ read mainly by the rich and the powerful, was saying rather patronisingly in an article about Lancashire football fans, 'Oop for Coop':

'The sturdy toilers, even if they wish above all things to see their own side win, have a real understanding of the nuances of scientific football.

'It is easy to understand why the Northern choirs are superior to those of

Football belongs to everybody

the South. When both are heard together during a prolonged episode of exiting play (during a match), the Northern basses and heavy baritones supply a pulsating drone-note in the fantasia of enthusiasm.

'They bring stone jars of strong ale and sandwiches an inch thick in little wicker baskets which can also be used for conveying carrier-pigeons.'

But the truth is that all classes, all kinds of people enjoy football and appreciate it. After all, the great game really started not in Scotland, as we so often think . . .

but in the public schools and universities of England and the real reason for the spread of soccer was in the enthusiasm of young men who came down from college to settle in the countryside as squires or parsons.

The pennyfarthing bicycle linked village to village and England, then Scotland, began to be a unified community, and the men who had played football at university taught the sport to the townsfolk and villagers.

That, then, was the start of organised Association Football.

Of course, the game had been played in a barbaric form for hundreds of years before the 1860's and 70's when football took its first real grip on the country.

It had been—as it still sometimes is—the subject of bitter controversy. For instance, in 1531, Thomas Elyot was writing: 'Footballe, wherein is nothinge but beastlie furie and extreme violence, whereof procedeth hurte and consequently rancour, and malice do remaine with them that be wounded; wherefore it is to be put in perpetuall silence.'

King and nobles were against the game because it interfered with practice at archery and the arts of war and, in 1314, a proclamation from London announced:

'Whereas our Lord the King is going towards the parts of Scotland, in his war against his enemies, and has especially commanded us strictly to keep his peace. . . . And whereas there is great uproar in the City, through certain tumults arising from great footballs in the fields of the public, from which many evils perchance may arise—which may God forbid—we do command and do forbid on the King's behalf, upon pain of imprisonment, that such game shall be not practised henceforth within the city.'

Football is JOY . . . and Partick Thistle players came off the field happy after they have won the League Cup at Hampden by beating Celtic.

94

Football is YOUTH's DREAM . . . and it's a dream come true for Charlie Brown, only 15 yet a member of a winning Morton team in a side against the mighty Celtic.

Football is GOALS . . . goals like this, scored by Celtic's Ken Dalglish against Ayr United.

The English should have stuck to football, then they might have escaped the humiliation of Bannockburn.

Yet the boys with the old school-ties and the gentry were those we must thank for giving us the game of soccer we know today. Later on, there were changes. And the 1880's marked a transitional period in the history of the game. Before the decade was over, the traditional, gentlemanly (and, believe me, far, far tougher) football of the ex-public schoolboys was to disappear from the playing fields, being superseded by the subtleties and skills of the professional performers who valued their limbs as stock-in-trade and got their effects by cunning rather than, as Denzil Batchelor, football's best historian once wrote, 'the unquestioning zeal of those who modelled themselves on the Light Brigade'.

But if that decade marked the end of the Old Boy supremacy as players, it certainly did not bring about the finish of the interest of ALL classes in the game.

And today, with football again far removed even from the new polished style of the early 1900's, with more thought going into the game, it is loved with equal enthusiasm by the mechanic and the minister, the pit-head worker and the priest, the barman and the barrister, the riveter and the royal.

What, then, is there about football that makes it the greatest sport in the world?

The Bishop of Norwich, who is an Arsenal supporter, says: 'After many years watching the game, I am only just beginning to see something of the pattern of the game and understand its intellectual flow.

'I'm still in my infancy in the matter but I can get pleasure from watching Charlie George, apparently wandering about aimlessly, yet waiting for his moment to fit into the pattern.

'Football is really a highly thoughtful game.'

Not only bishops love the game. Politicians, judges, industrialists are all to be seen in the stands.

Perhaps the Professor of Logic at Oxford University, Fred Ayer, who should know, sums up the attraction of football best. He says: 'It's the excitement. I'm no different from any other fan. There are moments of genuine aesthetic excitement rising from a piece of good play.'

John Cohen, Professor of Psychology, Manchester University: 'The appeal lies in the tension—the uncertainty, the drama, what's going to happen next when so many factors are involved.

'It's the delight in the physical exuberance, the agility and skill of the players whose minds work through their bodies and their toes.

'I can see nothing bad in the tension, so long as it is kept within the bounds and individual spectators don't become part of an anonymous and possibly violent mob.' We mustn't forget, however, that football is still only a sport and too many of us are inclined to think football is everything, a way of life, a religion.

It was the benign Percy M. Young, football's enchanting writer, who probably summed up the lure of the game best when he said:

'At a match, the only adults present seem to be the referee and linesmen, appearing, as they always do, grim and schoolmasterly.

'Football, whether for performers or spectators, renews childhood. Instinctively, we return to what we were. We are serious about trivialities. But it is a great thing to be able to take seriously what is unimportant. When we can do this we can begin to take seriously what is important.'

Certainly there is no doubt that one of the appeals of soccer is that we can, on a Saturday afternoon, find ourselves. We may be meek, polite, ready always to compromise for six days of the week. But on Saturdays we can let off steam, releasing tension.

Alas, no words can ever truthfully portray what football means to those who love it.

Let's just say it's the game that switches us on, the rich and the poor, the clever and the stupid, the long and the short and the tall.

THE LEGEND OF DIXIE DEANS (2)

Nowhere does the wheel of fortune fluctuate so swiftly and so dramatically as in football. That's why they say you're only as good as your last game. That's why a player knows he can, within seconds, change in the opinion of the crowd from hero to villain. Jeers follow cheers with the speed of a jet. And vice versa. Because soccer luck goes up and down with the rapidity of a liftman's nightmare.

This was proved to the hilt in the Scottish Cup Final of May 6, 1972, between Celtic and Hibernian at Hampden.

There was the story of Dixie Deans, the Celtic striker, whose world only 18 days before had crashed round his head. Dixie missed a penalty kick in the circus act that was the sad finale to his club's European Cup semi-final with Inter Milan.

Deans was soccer's saddest man for after two games, extra time and no goals the Italians won the penalty knock-out test.

Then came the Scottish Cup Final. . . .

There was the story of Hibernian, going places, on top of the world after a splendid victory over Rangers in the semi-final. Everyone in Edinburgh was convinced that Hibs were great again, would win cheers all the way down

Princes Street after the game by holding the cup aloft in their bus.

Then came the final. . . .

* * *

Before the big game, the prospects were summed up best—as always—by Celtic manager Jock Stein, who was confident the fans would see 'a good game of football'. He added: 'Finals at home nowadays are all too often the qualifying matches for something bigger and that means great tension but this time both Celtic and Hibernian have already qualified for Europe next season so there is no outside pressure.

'And when Celtic and Rangers meet there is worry and heat, so much so that it is difficult to get the football going, but a final with Celtic or Rangers against another club has always a chance of being a good game.'

Both clubs had much to play for. Celtic were desperately keen to finish the season successfully. They had won the League championship, they had been defeated finalists in the League Cup, but they had lost, technically, at least, in the European Cup and they wanted to roar to success at Hampden.

Stein had won seven successive League flags but never the Scottish Cup in suc-

Celtic skipper Billy McNeill gets the first goal in the Scottish Cup final against Hibernian at Hampden, and shows how it feels to be a scorer.

cessive years. Celtic had, however the best Scottish Cup record of any team in Scotland, having won the trophy 21 times and lost in the final on 13 occasions.

Hibs, 97 years old, had last won the Cup in 1902—at Parkhead when they beat Celtic 1–0 in the final. They had won it only once previously and that was in 1887 when they triumphed over Dumbarton 2–1. Six times they had been losing finalists between 1896 and 1958.

Hibernian's high hopes of better days to come started with the signing as manager of Eddie Turnbull, one of the Famous Five attack of Easter Road's glorious days, but latterly renowned as a brilliantly successful manager with Aberdeen. And he had done tremendously well since returning to Easter Road, hastening success by strengthening the team with Jim Herriot in goal, Alex Edwards in midfield and Alan Gordon in the attack.

Hibs were playing progressive, exciting football—but Celtic were still the favourites. The teams had reached the final like this:

First round: Celtic 5, Albion Rovers 0; Partick Thistle 0, Hibs 2; Second Round: Celtic 4, Dundee 0; Hibs 2, Airdrie 0; Third round: Celtic 1, Hearts 1, replay 0–1; Hibs 2, Aberdeen 0; Semi-final: Celtic 3, Kilmarnock 1; Rangers 1, Hibs 1; replay 2–0.

It promised to be a great game.

But no-one realised just how spectacular it was going to be—for Celtic. . . .

*   *   *

A crowd of 106,102 turned up at Hampden on a typical Scottish May day, bright now and again with glimpses of sunshine but with clouds always threatening rain.

The line-up was:

Celtic: Williams, Craig, Brogan, Murdoch, McNeill, Connelly, Johnstone, Deans, Macari, Dalglish, Callaghan. Substitute: Lennox. Hibernian: Herriot, Brownlie, Schaedler, Stanton, Black, Blackley, Edwards, Hazel, Gordon, O'Rourke, Duncan. Substitute: Auld.

Referee: A. MacKenzie, Larbert.

The start was sensational—mainly because of that special Celtic magic. Hibs defenders blinked when they saw that wee Jimmy Johnstone was operating on the left touchline—and their worries started at once.

This was when Celtic laid the foundations of victory, in the opening minutes. They began to string together a series of splendid passes. Hibs were spinning.

In just over two minutes, Celtic scored, hitting hard and quickly. Johnstone was fouled by an anxious Hibernian defender. Jim Brogan took the free-kick. Skipper Billy McNeill sidled up and Alan Gordon's covering was loose. Brogan placed the ball and, to a great Celtic roar, McNeill strode forward to smash the easy shot into the net.

Then, to their eternal credit, Hibernian hit back. Instead of being upset by such a tragic start, Eddie Turnbull's men played bravely and eagerly. It was Celtic's turn to become nervous. After only 12 minutes, Hibernian equalised with a fine move which stretched more than half the length of the pitch.

Young Hazel started it with a square pass to sweeper John Blackley. This set the whole team in motion. The ball was pushed forward to Arthur Duncan, thus giving him clear space to use his speed for the first time in the match.

The left-winger hared to the byeline, measured a low cross perfectly and the Celtic defence were flustered. They could only watch Gordon slide the ball over the line after goalkeeper Williams and left-back Brogan had made touches

The hero of Hampden can relax. Dixie Deans is congratulated by keeper Evan Williams and trainer Neilly Mochan at the Cup final.

which were not enough to clear the danger.

And now the cup final began to boil and it turned into as good a game as even old grey Hampden had ever seen.

But it was Celtic who took the initiative.

Released into the midfield, Johnstone began to impress his unique talents on a match which was embroidered everywhere with skill and pace.

Then the Hibs defence were slack again in defence—and the legend of Dixie Deans, the new, happy legend of Deans, began. In 24 minutes he put Celtic ahead with a goal strangely similar to his team's opening score. Again Johnstone was fouled. Bobby Murdoch judged his curling free kick to the inch and Deans headed beautifully into the net.

Top man in Europe

And Celtic began to turn on the style.

Murdoch was immense, the best middle-man in Europe. Hibs began to falter and it was as well for them that John Blackley was in fine form, ably assisted by centre-half Jim Black. But the attractive football came from Celtic. McNeill had the Easter Road attack subdued and only Duncan, in spasms, looked menacing.

Hibernian had a promising surge of spirit and skill at the start of the second half when they started to play as they had played against Rangers in the semi-final replay. But Celtic settled the final with one of the most unusual and most skilful goals ever known in a cup final.

It started with an astonishingly accurate pass from Murdoch which let Lou Macari away. Deans caught his colleague's pass near the byeline. He seemed hemmed in, with no friendly foot to pass to and only inches of the pitch to use.

Then Dixie became Celtic's hero.

*   *   *

He turned past Brownlie. Then he dummied Blackley. Then he sent goalkeeper Herriot the wrong way. Twice he beat the keeper and when it seemed he had held on too long he sent the ball sliding into the net to a joyful ovation. It was supreme skill on a sixpence, a goal of goals. Dixie said later that he thought he had lost the ball a couple of times. It was the goal of a lifetime, though, a goal that, if it had been notched in England, would have been repeated hundreds of times as 'goal of the season'.

The goal came at a vital time for Celtic. For Hibs were having their best period of the match, looking as though they could equalise.

Anyhow, it was the decisive goal. After 65 minutes, Duncan, the most dangerous Edinburgh attacker, collapsed and left the field on a stretcher. On came Bertie Auld, a great former Celt, and well though he played against his old mates he couldn't turn the tide.

Fifteen minutes from time, the bell tolled finally for Hibs. A long Callaghan pass found Deans unmarked and Dixie carried the ball on, drew Herriot off his line and then pushed the ball into the net for a great hat-trick.

Hibs tried to come back in the only way possible—storming. For Celtic had outplayed them in football. Yet no matter how Hibs hurled themselves at Williams's goal they made no impact.

A moment of glory for Hibernian. Alan Gordon scores their only Scottish Cup Final goal.

With seven minutes to go Celtic scored a magnificent fifth goal. Callaghan's fine pass let Craig away. The back, who was playing his last game for Celtic before going to South Africa, sent the ball over and Macari swung smoothly at it to score brilliantly.

Hibs had been run into the ground and, near the end, Macari scored his second and Celtic's sixth in what had been a memorable final.

*　　*　　*

Celtic had become the first team this century to score six goals in a Scottish Cup Final—and only the second in all history. The other club were Renton, away back in 1888.

Yet Hibs take praise and the incredible truth is that for more than an hour it was a tremendous final, contested between two teams of rare talent.

In that hour Celtic had the edge but there was no hint of the total superiority that was to come the Parkhead way in the end.

It was a pity the second half was marred by fighting and feuding on the terracing, with hundreds running on to the track to seek safety as the bottles and beer cans flew.

Perhaps soon we will have a Scottish Cup Final staged as spectacularly as that in England. Now it is just another game, with not sufficient done to turn it into a great occasion.

For Deans, however, it was his most wonderful day in football. According to the record books, the last time a hat-trick was scored in the final was in 1904 when Jimmy Quinn scored all his team's goals in Celtic's 3–2 win over Rangers. Another interesting point was that after playing for Renton in that other 6–1 result last century Jim Kelly went on to become the first captain of the first Celtic team. He was father of the late Sir Robert Kelly, Celtic's most famous chairman.

For Hibs, it was a sad afternoon but they are a young team and they would come back.

They could remember Deans, remember that for young men who entertain millions with their skills elation invariably follows frustration. Such is the fascination of football.

*　　*　　*

But what most people wanted to know was—what is the magic that makes Celtic?

There's a potent compound in the spell over Parkhead. Perseverance is one ingredient. Jock Stein is another. For he is the master of tactics, an inspiration, a dream manager.

Versatility, resilience, imagination, pace, power—all these, too, play a part in Celtic's magical roundabout.

Abroad, they catch their breath, the Continental experts, and tell you: 'Ah, Celtic are so fast, so unusual in attack, so strong'.

My view is that Celtic are at the top mainly because they continue a rich heritage; they have more artistic, *thinking* players than most. The Parkhead formula doesn't actually change.

In the great old Celtic days, the heroes were the McGrorys, the Quinns, the Delaneys—the flamboyant, extrovert, dashing scorers who made the headlines.

But these stars couldn't have been the lethal finishers they became without the aid of the man of genius, the astute wing-half and inside-forward of craft, cunning and superb control. Patsy Gallagher, Alex Thomson, Malcolm MacDonald, Peter Wilson. These were some of the elegant ball players whose skill set the Celtic pattern.

And so it is today. Jimmy Johnstone is a wonder of the touchline, often top of the bill. But always making the play, sometimes behind the scenes, are Bobby Murdoch and George Connelly, technically perfect in today's crisper soccer but certainly players who would have fitted in brilliantly to the courtlier scene of yesteryear.

Murdoch is known as one of the most brilliant mid-field players of all time. Connelly is a tall young man who may well become as famous as Beckenbauer of Germany.

It took the genius of Stein to give Connelly a new role, an unusual role. In the old days, he would naturally have become what we called 'a silken half-back with the velvet touch'. Today he directs from behind.

Not only does he work a fine partnership with Billy McNeill as a double centre-back; he *makes* play often from his own penalty area with superlative passes.

For Connelly is a princely player, a creative player, even though his main platform is in the rear.

Thus the Celtic magic may be glimpsed, if never matched. Some club may find a new Stein. Another a new Johnstone, Murdoch or Connelly. Or a Deans. But who had them all together, at the time of the final?

Only Celtic.

Celtic took the gilt of the past and welded it to the chrome of modern soccer, embellishing it with that special magic of their own.

Now we can only hope that Hibernian will go on trying to find the magic that keeps Parkhead fans in a trance of delight—and make themselves stern challengers to the Celts.

Scenes we could do without. Trouble breaks out in the Cup Final crowd at Hampden.

Oh, those marvellous memories

The great moments in football are fleeting. In a second or less, a marvellous goal can be scored, a dreadful mistake made.

Yet the great moments live on, the moments of triumph, of tragedy.

Many games you can forget thankfully.

But there are always the magic moments, etched in the mind of the fan for ever. And sometimes, the camera helps us to recall the glowing incidents in football's pageantry. . . .

Like these. . . .

He's obviously not one of the streamlined heroes of today's soccer. The outfit shows that the picture wasn't taken last season—or the season before that. A giant of the past, you say?

Of course, he was. But he's also the giant of today, the greatest figure in Scottish football.

That's right.

He's Jock Stein.

This picture of Jock in action for Celtic was taken on a winter's day at Falkirk . . . in the 1950s.

It was 20 years ago that Jock joined Celtic, to begin his momentous association with the club.

On December 4, 1951, he arrived, unhailed, practically unheard of, at Parkhead. No headlines. No hordes to welcome him. No singing and dancing in the Parkhead streets.

All the papers said was: "Celtic have concluded a deal with Llanelly, a Welsh non-League club, for their centre-half, Jock Stein, who had been with Albion Rovers."

The fans were hardly impressed, either. Celtic were struggling and many considered that they should have signed a goal-scorer not a defender, who was hardly in the highest class.

Stein made his first appearance for Celtic four days later against St. Mirren at Parkhead. And right away it was admitted that he brought steadiness to the defence. That was the simple start of the Stein saga, probably the most wonderful story in football, certainly the story Celtic fans love best.

Stein not only took Celtic out of trouble on the playing field. He took them to glory undreamed of, to European Cup triumph, to unsurpassed success in Scotland. It was sad, however, that last season, too, the man who brought Stein to Celtic died—Sir Robert Kelly, one of football's most famous legislators.

Few men at the top did more for the game than Sir Robert, Celtic's most renowned chairman, who was also president of the Scottish League and SFA.

He was a magnificent legislator because he knew football better than most. The game was the love of his life. He will be sadly missed. But his work for the club and for football will never be forgotten.

For Kilmarnock, it wasn't a season really to remember. It was a season of transition. Once Kilmarnock were great, doughty cup-fighters, League champions. But they were rebuilding and often things didn't go as planned.

Killie, though, have a great tradition. And they showed up the critics in a fine Scottish Cup run last season. This is a moment of glory for wee Jim Cook, a smashing wee winger. He shows his joy after scoring against Raith Rovers in a Scottish Cup-tie at Kirkcaldy.

My chance came true on my own doorstep

by ARCHIE KNOX
Dundee United.

A surveyor before
he became a full-
time footballer with
his new club.

It took me six years and two transfers to
finish on my own doorstep and realise a
soccer ambition I suppose I held since
the time I first kicked a tennis ball round
a school playground.

Born and bred in Dundee, it had
always been my goal to play for one or
other of the local teams. But at one time
not so long ago it had seemed like the one
goal I would never score.

After five years with little Forfar Athletic, I got the chance to move. But not to
Dundee or Dundee United. Instead, I

moved right out of the area. To Love Street and St. Mirren.

Don't get the idea that I wasn't happy to go to Paisley. It was a step in the right direction and the 20-odd games I had for them in the First Division were great experience.

And, oddly enough, the match I shall always remember as the most exciting, the most enjoyable of my career, had the most tragic consequences.

We met Celtic at Love Street in our last League game needing a victory to stay in the First Division. It seemed out of our reach, especially as Celtic wanted points to clinch their sixth successive League championship.

It was a classic case of David and Goliath in soccer. But how close we came to shaking Jock Stein's men. How close we came to staying up that April evening.

Twice we edged our way into the lead, raised our hopes, and silenced the big Celtic support that had followed to Love Street.

However, it wasn't to be. They hit back twice to equalise and we went into the Second Division. I suppose it should have been a sickening occasion for me after just half-a-season in the big League.

But, don't ask me why, I'll always treasure the memory of that game above all others.

I'll always remember, too, the day I came home to Dundee by signing for United.

They weren't doing so well at the time, struggling near the foot of the League. But, despite having already suffered the agony of relegation, I didn't have to be asked twice if I would sign the forms that saw me fulfil an ambition.

It wasn't just a case of joining one of my favourite clubs, of course. The move

also gave me the chance to go full-time at last and give up my job as a surveyor with Dundee Corporation.

Being full-time just has to be the aim of every part-timer in the game. It had certainly always been mine. It is only when you concentrate all energies and time to football that you know for sure how good you can be.

On this score I couldn't have joined a better club than United. Because I cannot rate manager Jim McLean too highly.

He has the great knack of pushing players to get the most out of them without losing their respect in any way. That must be half the battle for any manager.

Although the team struggled through last season I am sure the boss will make things happen for United in time. He is too deeply involved in the game, too interested, for anything else to happen.

I hope I am part of the new United . . . I hope I can hit some of the goals that help the club back to the top. But not as an out-and-out striker.

Right from the start of my senior career at Station Park I have enjoyed coming forward from the middle of the park to have a crack at goal. And I find I get more goals that way than by playing forward all the time.

That is something no-one can explain, I reckon. Perhaps it is just that, having the knowledge that some other guy should be getting the goals makes it a bit easier on players like me to pop the occasional one into the back of the net.

Once you gain the reputation for being a top striker people can expect too much. You begin to try too hard . . . and that is when things go wrong. That is when shots go everywhere but the back of the net.

THEY'RE THE PRIDE OF SCOTLAND

The old and the young, the short and the tall, the slim and the stocky—Scotland is rich in players of all kinds. They come in all sizes. That's why Scotland is still the envy of the football world, the small country which produces star after star.

They're still coming up, lads of rare distinction—and they are helped on their way to the top by players who have already established themselves.

Here are just a few of the Scottish footballers who have earned the cheers recently....

JIM COOK (Kilmarnock)....Oh, what a rare wee winger!

KEN MACKIE (Dunfermline Athletic) . . . what a future's in front of this 16-year-old.

SANDY JARDINE (Rangers) . . . a Ranger of today in the mould of the Ibrox greats of yesteryear

My lucky break — a free transfer from Celtic!

by KENNY AIRD
ST JOHNSTONE

When I tell you about three of the best things that have happened in my football career you'll probably think I'm off my head. Just give me a chance to explain.

The first good break I got was being FREED by Celtic. Yes, let go by the greatest Scottish club of all!

The second was, believe it or not, being a St. Mirren player when they were relegated to the Second Division.

The third was being left out of the St. Johnstone side for a spell last season. Yes, I got a break by being dropped.

Now let me explain these statements fully before every Celtic, St. Mirren and St. Johnstone fan in the country gets the wrong idea about Kenny Aird.

First, Celtic, the club I joined from

Like life itself, football never moves smoothly. Kenny Aird knows that better than most—for he has had his fair share of ups and downs.

Drumchapel Amateurs when I was just 16. At the time it seemed like a dream come true. But it wasn't.

I soon realised that Celtic had so many good players on their books that I would have to stick around for years before I ever smelled a chance to play in the first team.

I stuck it for a year and wasn't particularly upset when they told me I could go.

From Parkhead I went to St. Mirren ... for my first taste of a regular place in a First Division side.

Happy times for Kenny Aird as he jokes with St Johnstone colleagues at the station.

I really enjoyed the taste. But it didn't last. After two seasons we found ourselves at the bottom of the League and relegated. I didn't know it at the time but relegation helped me a whole lot.

For, while I was getting used to the idea of having to play in the Second Division, St. Johnstone manager Willie Ormond came along with a close-season offer.

The fact that Mr. Ormond was a fair old winger himself as a player with Hibs and Scotland has had a great influence on my career.

He understands the problems of being a little man out to make a big impression. Right through his career he displayed courage both on the park and off it.

And last season, when he decided to drop me, I had to admit eventually that he knew exactly what had gone wrong with my game.

I was doing everything right apart from making my final pass pay off. I'd fly down the wing, beat my man as well as ever and then . . . nothing.

I was a bit stunned when he took me aside and told me I was out of the first team. I felt a bit hurt.

But, when I sat down and thought about it, he was dead right. The more I thought the more anxious I became to sort myself out and get on with the game as it should be played.

The result was amazing. When my chance came to return to the side—because of the long list of injuries that struck us last season—I was a new player. I don't consider I am boasting when I say I had my best-ever season.

The highlights of the season came in Europe. When I left Parkhead I thought I'd probably never get the chance to tackle top clubs abroad. But, after several disappointments, Saints managed to win a place in the UEFA Cup.

We couldn't have had a tougher start, being drawn against SV Hamburg in the opening round. Even our staunchest supporters didn't give us much of a chance. They felt they would see one European tie at Muirton and that would be it.

When we went out to meet them in the first leg in Hamburg I felt that our fans were probably right. The Germans seemed to have too many big names for the unknowns from Perth.

At the end of 90 minutes I had second thoughts. We had played brilliantly at times and gone down by just 2–1.

The return at Muirton will always have a special place in my soccer memories. The big crowd—something we rarely see apart from our games with Rangers and Celtic—drove us on wonderfully. We thrashed Hamburg 3–0.

Our next tie, against Vasas, of Hungary, was just as dramatic, and it made me realise that there is more to being a winger than beating a full-back and getting the ball into the middle.

We were up against it after winning the first leg by just 2–0. But Mr. Ormond planned brilliantly for the return. We held out until just before the end to qualify 2–1 on aggregate.

My role that afternoon was to chase back, win the ball and hold it as long as possible. It was a negative game but I enjoyed every minute of it.

Our dreams of glory in Europe ended in the third round when Zel Sarajevo thrashed us 5–2 on aggregate. In fact, the whole thing nearly ended for the entire party when our plane almost crashed on the way home.

But we got back safely . . . and I wouldn't let that narrow escape hold me back if I get another chance to play in Europe.

Through MUD, through SNOW

Yes, through mud, through snow, through blinding rain . . . football goes on. Certainly you can't be a fairweather man if you want to be a soccer star nowadays.

So spare a thought for the players, match officials—and the photographers who took these intriguing pictures—as we look back on some of the shocking Saturdays on which football was played last season.

STAND-IN IN THE SNOW. . . . Why did I ever make a comeback? That seems to be what Jack Mowat is thinking as he patrols the line at Cappielow. Jack was once one of our outstanding referees. Now he's a supervisor. But it was back to duty as a linesman during an emergency at Greenock. He might have chosen a better day. . . .

ANGER IN THE MUD. . . . Rangers' classy winger Tommy McLean grits his teeth and tries to keep his cool after an incident in a match at Shawfield with Clyde's John McHugh. Hardly mud larks here . . . more a matter of mud sparks.

JOY IN THE MUD. . . . Falkirk
players go wild with delight after
scoring against Rangers on a
muddy surface in a Scottish
Cup-tie.

HERO IN THE MUD . . . that's Partick Thistle's brilliant goalkeeper, Alan Rough, to whom it doesn't matter whether it's snowing or raining, whether the pitch is muddy or firm; he usually turns in a tremendous performance.

DRAMA IN THE DRIFT....
Rangers centre-forward Colin
Stein receives attention after he
has found himself stuck in the net
in the middle of winter.

SPLASHING THROUGH. . . .
Aberdeen's Davie Robb skims
past Hearts' Eddie Thomson, who
seems waterlogged in torrential
rain, during a match at Tynecastle.

120

THANKS, BROTHER

by DUNCAN LAMBIE
Dundee

'Big brother is watching you.' By 1984 that phrase might be enough to frighten footballers and anyone else for that matter. But not Duncan Lambie.

You see, my big brother John, the St. Johnstone full-back, has been the biggest single influence on my career. I can thank him for most of the good things that have happened to me.

From the time I was old enough to kick my first tanner ba' John has kept an eye on my progress. He has always been around to encourage, tick off and advise.

We train together whenever we have the chance and, after these sessions, I always feel I have learned something new. I cannot thank him enough for that.

I suppose I would have been delighted to join his club when my chance came to go senior. But, although that didn't happen, John still had a lot to do with my signing for Dundee.

One Wednesday night in 1971, while I was with Armadale Juniors, I was invited to play a trial for Rangers at Ibrox—against Dundee.

In the game, I did enough to impress Rangers sufficiently to be asked to play another trial. But John Prentice, Dundee's manager at that time, was impressed, too.

He had known me as a bootboy with Falkirk during his days as boss at Brockville. He had filed my name away in his mind for future reference.

So, instead of another Ranger trial, I found myself turning out for Dundee Reserves just five days later. This time I really grabbed my chance by banging in two goals against Aberdeen's second string.

Mr Prentice had me in his office right after the game. I talked to him . . . to my brother John . . . and signed on the dotted line an hour later.

If John didn't exactly convince me that night that I had made the right move, I didn't have long to wait for the real proof. For, just a couple of weeks later, I made my first team debut.

Last season, of course, I came to be accepted as a first team regular. It wasn't all easy going, full of glowing memories, but I learned a lot and enjoyed a lot.

The games I'll really remember were our UEFA Cup battles with Cologne and AC Milan . . . even though I feel I was robbed when we played against the Germans over there.

With the score 0–0 and Dundee getting on top, I broke away from their World Cup defender Wolfgang Weber and cracked a shot into the back of the net. I thought I was made. But the referee ruled no goal—although I'll never know why.

Still, if that goal had counted, we might have strolled through the tie and robbed our own fans of their greatest night in years.

After losing the first leg 2–1, we slid f u r t h e r   b e h i n d — 4 – 2   o n aggregate—with just 20 minutes of the return match left. We were 99 per cent out of Europe.

Then : . . 1 . . . 2 . . . 3. We hit the Germans with three glorious goals that brought the house down, got us through 5–4 on aggregate, and left 15,500 fans limp with excitement. A few players and fans left Dens that night with tears of joy in their eyes!

The next round did not have such a happy ending for Dundee. But we did far better than most people expected after losing 3–0 in Italy.

Mr Prentice ordered us to play the second-leg as a good old fashioned

Scottish Cup tie. How close we came to showing these proud Italians just how good Scottish football can be.

I managed to lay on the first goal for Gordon Wallace despite almost having the shirt torn off my back. Then, in the second-half, I hit the post from 20 yards and John Duncan netted the rebound. 2–3.

After that we made a mockery of AC Milan's reputation for being masters of ice-cool defence. They kicked the ball anywhere like a bunch of frightened amateurs.

We could not get that third goal that would have pushed the tie into extra time but, even in defeat, I remember that game as the one in which I arrived as a Dundee player . . . a proud one at that.

122   **John Lamblie, St. Johnstone—'I owe him a vote of thanks,' says Duncan.**

Second again — but the Dandy Dons battle on

No-one ever remembers who was second. That's one of the sad and brutal facts of this sporting life. And with Celtic making history in season 1971–72 by winning the Scottish League championship for a record-breaking seventh time in a row, few people outside the granite city realised just what a fine job Aberdeen did in keeping the title race alive.

It was the second season in succession that the Dons finished runners-up to Celtic, hardly an enviable achievement. But if it hadn't been for the tenacious and durable Aberdeen the league would have ended in a runaway Celtic triumph.

So the Scottish football public owe Aberdeen a hearty vote of thanks.

This may seem strange coming from me for I have been accused of criticising Aberdeen too severely. Perhaps I have—but that does not prevent me from complimenting the men from the north on keeping the League challenge alive.

Aberdeen were not the most popular team in Scotland. The reason for that is because the average Scottish fan at heart relishes the spectacular attacking play, the style that calls for splendid wing raids, rollicking aggression and elegant, imaginative moves.

That's why Celtic are the toast not only of their own legions of devoted fans but of the neutrals who love football that brings excitement and glamour.

But Aberdeen?

Aberdeen are different. Aberdeen are the professionals. Cool, unflustered, deadly, masters of their trade. Feared. But hardly loved.

Aberdeen are the moderns in Scotland. They are like the top professionals in other spheres. For the professionals today have to be so good, so ruthless that the one thing they can't do, or even afford to do, is win friends and influence people.

Several times, indeed, the Dons were booed and slowhandclapped away from home. But they received this treatment simply due to the fact that they are the most flexible, best-drilled and modernly methodical team in the country.

And that, as I've said, is something Aberdeen must live with because the Scottish legend dies hard—the legend that our native football is a brisk, artistic game, won by strokes of breath-taking genius, unsullied by devices and styles taken from abroad.

Aberdeen are something completely

different. Their style derives from many countries—the economy of Italy, the hard-hitting attacks of West Germany, the work-rate and remorseless covering of Russia.

Their trouble is that their style is so well designed, so carefully planned that it is anything but flamboyant, planned, in fact, to be accident-proof more than goal-explosive.

That doesn't appeal to many Scottish fans. Especially as the Dons are also accused of exploiting an offside trap. That makes me laugh. Offside is part of the game and it is usually the ineptness of opposing forwards more than the offside tactics of the defenders that lead to frustrated jeers from the crowd.

But the hard truth is that Aberdeen could not play the way they do without having first-class players. And although they transferred their cool captain, Martin Buchan, to Manchester United, much to the annoyance of many of their supporters, they still have a pool of brilliant talent, including goalkeeper Bobby Clark, the promising centre-half Willie Young, the persevering Steve Murray, flashing winger Arthur Graham and goal-snatcher-de-luxe Joe Harper.

Now they have added fine forwards in Drew Jarvie, from Airdrie, and Barrie Mitchell, from Dunfermline.

Whether, having been second twice, Aberdeen feel they may have to change

Bobby Clark—Aberdeen's brilliant goalkeeper.

Matches between Celtic and Aberdeen are always highlights of the season. Here's a thrilling duel, with Aberdeen's powerful Davie Robb and Celtic's Bobby Murdoch.

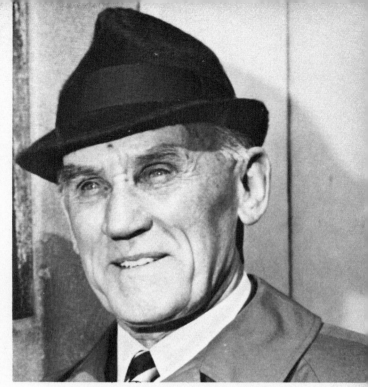

The Chief Scout—that's what they call Aberdeen's top talent-spotter, Bobby Calder, who has put so many youngsters on the path to fame

their style, I don't know. I don't think they will. Whether the fans like it or not, it brings variety to the Scottish soccer scene—and variety is essential in a league in which there are all too few challengers.

Aberdeen may well say that their motto is: It's easy to be popular—but it's a damn sight harder to be champions.

If they are to win the title, their dearest ambition—and something they've done only once, in 1954–55—they will, however, need even more good players. That's why the big fee they received from Buchan was used to reinforce their pool.

Says the shrewd, likeable manager, Jimmy Bonthrone: 'We need more and more good players. A big pool is the real

The man who left—Martin Buchan, is one of the best sweepers in the business—and Aberdeen fans weren't too happy when he was transferred to Manchester United.

secret of success in this modern age.'

He appreciates that Celtic can freshen their team every week—but he does not regard it as mere chance that Jock Stein has so many good players eager to challenge for a regular first-team place. He knows that the pool of Celtic players has been fashioned with rare skill from their great resources of money, popularity

Tragedy for Celtic—but a break for the Dons. Celtic skipper Billy McNeill holds his hands to his face after scoring against his own team in a vital game with Aberdeen.

One of Aberdeen's most promising players is giant centre-half Willie Young, seen battling with Celtic's Lou Macari.

and advantageous geographical position in the centre of the West of Scotland's industrial belt.

'So,' goes on Jimmy Bonthrone, 'we must search even wider, even harder for players who can come into the first team when the regulars are injured or stale'.

Aberdeen are ambitious. With their city the centre of the new oil boom, they can look for even more enthusiastic support. But they must go on winning.

They have come a long way from modest beginnings away back in 1903. Before then, the football reputation of the north-east was in the hands of two clubs, Victoria United and Orion. Many of the best players in these two clubs were teachers and Orion at one time had no fewer than four headmasters in their ranks.

The scholastic profession, too, has played a big part in the distinguished progress of Aberdeen, who moved, in turn, from the Recreation Ground, the Holborn Cricket Ground and Chanonry Gardens to their fine stadium, Pittodrie, a fresh, lively place swept by the cool North Sea breezes.

In the old days, rugged, stalwart fellows, like the granite of the city, helped to carry the fortunes of the club—husky players such as Jock Hutton, one of Scotland's most serviceable backs, and Wilfred Low, a strong half-back.

But Aberdeen did not rely only on power. Soon they were noted for craft and artistry and one of their greatest personalities was Donald Colman, a dapper star from Maryhill Juniors in Glasgow, who conceived a new style for the Dons and earned fame abroad when he became one of the first Scottish coaches to migrate to the Continent.

Their best year was 1954–55 when they won the championship with consistent displays, losing only five games in the strenuous League programme and winning the flag with 49 points, scoring 73 goals and giving away only 26.

That was when they realised the value of top-class reserves. That was when they put the accent on teamwork.

And certainly teamwork won them their League flag.

There was a howl of protest that summer from north-east fans when the SFA announced the names of the 16 players to tour the Continent during the close season. Not one Aberdeen player was in the party and the fans were asking indignantly: 'Don't they know Aberdeen have just won the League?'

A closer analysis of the Dons' performance, however, emphasised the fact that their first-ever success was a triumph of team-work rather than anything else—and the selectors could hardly have chosen the complete Pittodrie eleven, brilliant though it was.

Another Aberdeen secret was—and still is—scouting. The Dons have an extensive scouting system, with the boss that outstanding spotter of talent, Bobby Calder, a former referee who is now recognised as probably Scotland's Chief Scout.

Well, Aberdeen know where they are going. They may still be booed. But they can look on that as an expression of admiration—for purposeful football.

It's always good to go north to see Aberdeen at Pittodrie. Few would grudge them another top triumph.